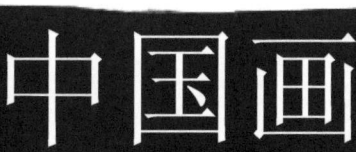

Traditional Chinese Art
An Introduction

BY
WAYNE M. MILLER

CONTENTS

Foreword

This is the introduction I wish I would have had when my curiosity first began with this enigmatic topic. The overview presented here is an excellent starting point for anyone interested in traditional Chinese art, Chinese culture or for those wanting to broaden their exposure to different mediums and styles of art.

I hope after viewing you will have a better understanding of the different parts involved in traditional Chinese art, resulting in a clearer way to reach your own goals and enjoyment of this subject.

~W.M.M. 卫世宁

中国画

Traditional Chinese Art
Presented in Three Parts

中国画 *zhong guo hua*	**Chinese Painting**
书法 *shu fa*	**Calligraphy**
印章 *yin zhang*	**Signet Seals**

Where it all begins
—
TOOLS OF THE TRADE

Traditional Chinese art requires a specialized set of equipment. Most important are the *Four Treasures:* brush, ink, paper and inkwell. Every studio, desk, and tea table that practices traditional Chinese art will have these items.

Each of the four treasures must be balanced with the other three. The quality of every implement has a direct result on the look, feel and finish of the artwork.

The quality of the utensils differs widely: cheap, expensive, and collector. Many of the high-end, well made products are works of art in themselves, handcrafted by specialized artisans.

文房四宝

wén fáng sì bao

The Four Treasures

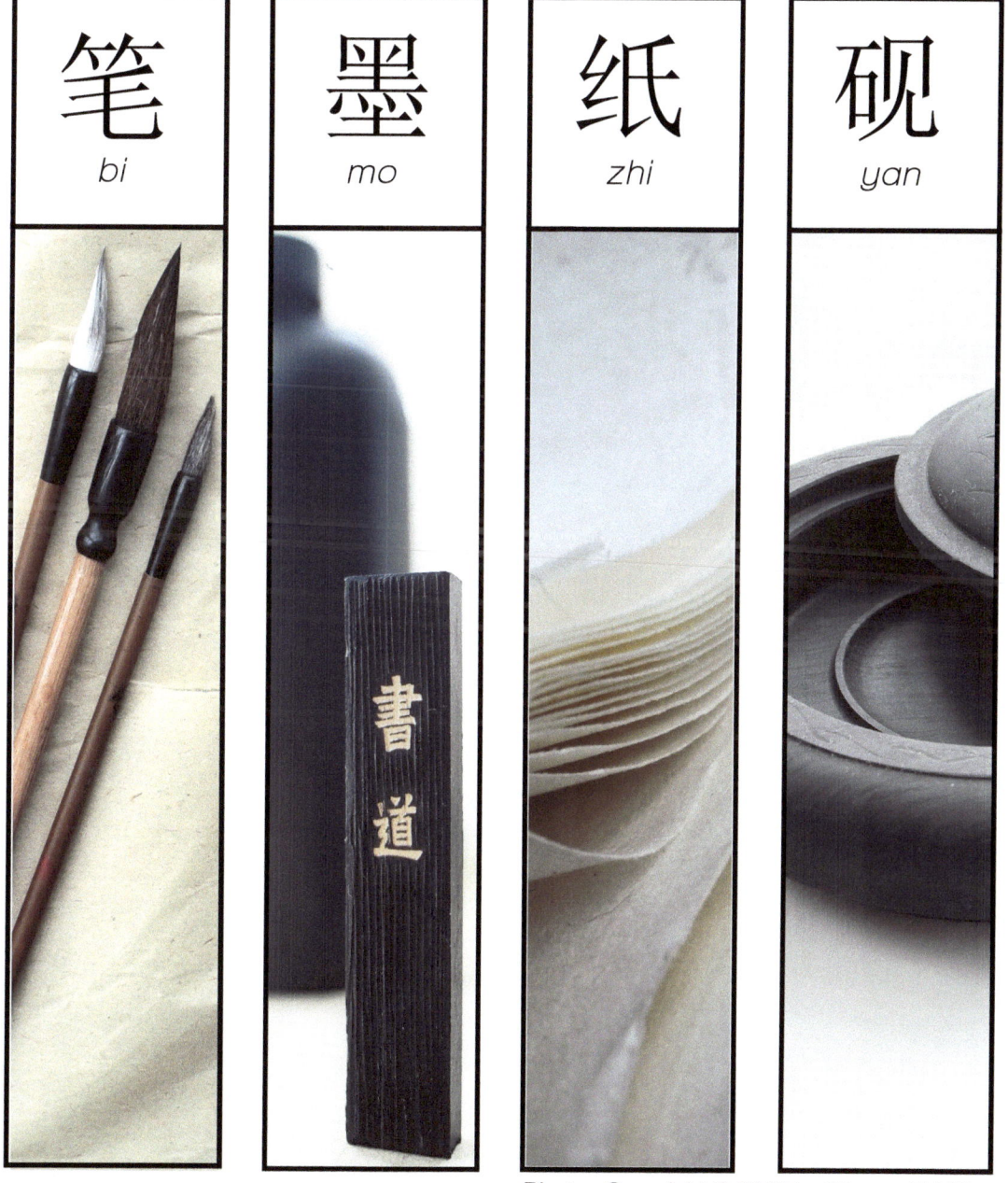

笔	墨	纸	砚
bi	*mo*	*zhi*	*yan*

Photos Copyright © 2015 by Wayne M Miller

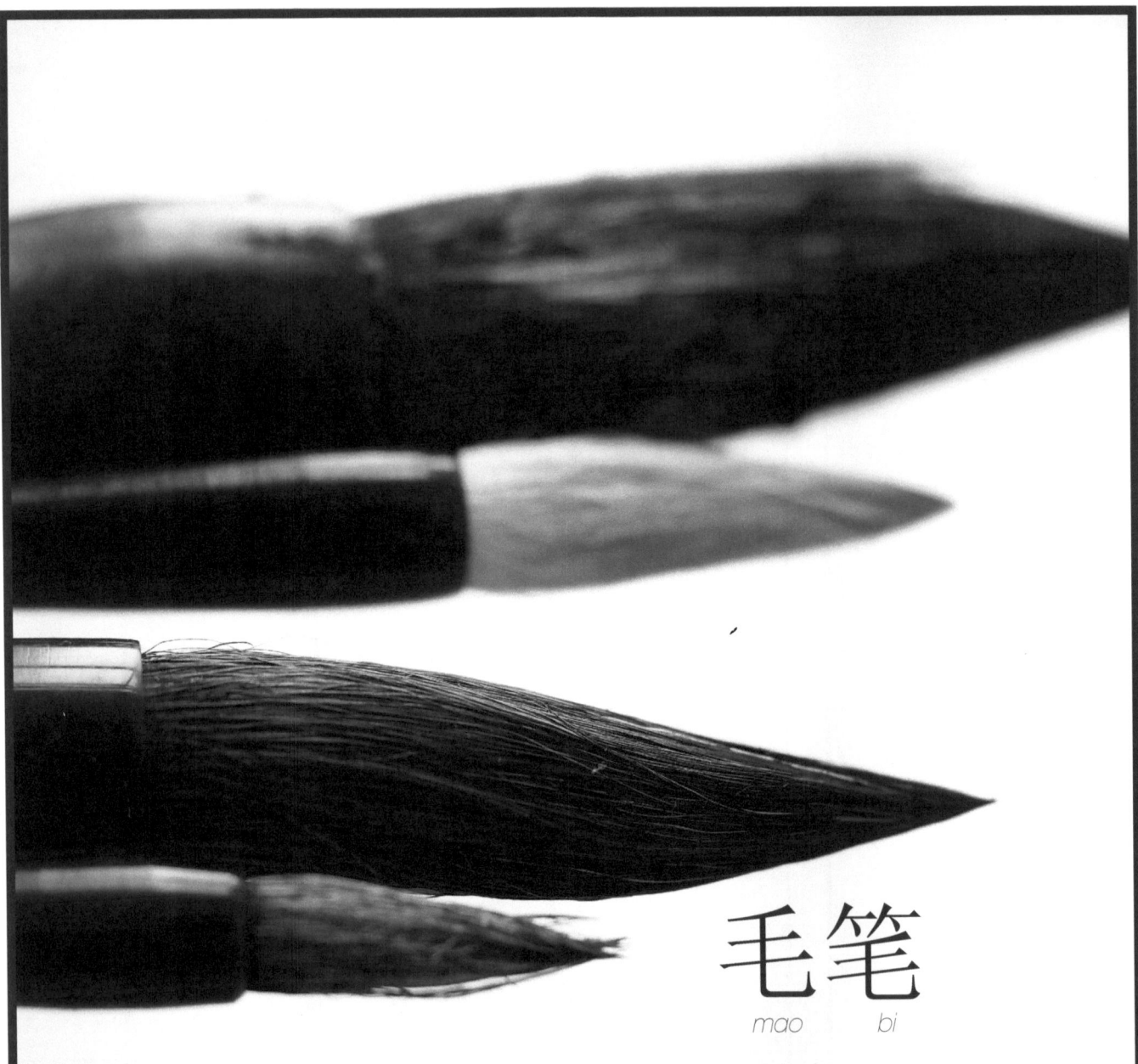

毛笔

mao   *bi*

Brushes used for Chinese art come in many sizes and varieties to suit different purposes. Bristles are composed of one or more kind of rabbit, goat, weasel, or other animal hair. Hair type is often mixed and specially arranged, creating the desired character for the brush, such as how it holds ink and whether it is soft or stiff.

When used, the brush is often thought of as an extension of the arm. This analogy brings to mind the importance of technique and the primary goal of every artist; mastering control of the brush.

Handles are made of wood or bamboo and typically include a classification:

SOFT	MIXED	STIFF
软毫	兼毫	硬毫
ruan hao	*jian hao*	*ying hao*

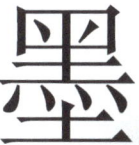

墨

mo

Like paper, ink was an expensive commodity in ancient China. Modern manufacturing has lowered prices and now ink can be bought in two forms, the traditional ink stick and bottled liquid ink.

Ink sticks are generally higher quality than liquid, having more depth and texture and being well suited for mixing to the desired shade in the ink stone.

Liquid ink is less expensive, therefore more desirable, when a large amount is needed, such as for practice or for calligraphy.

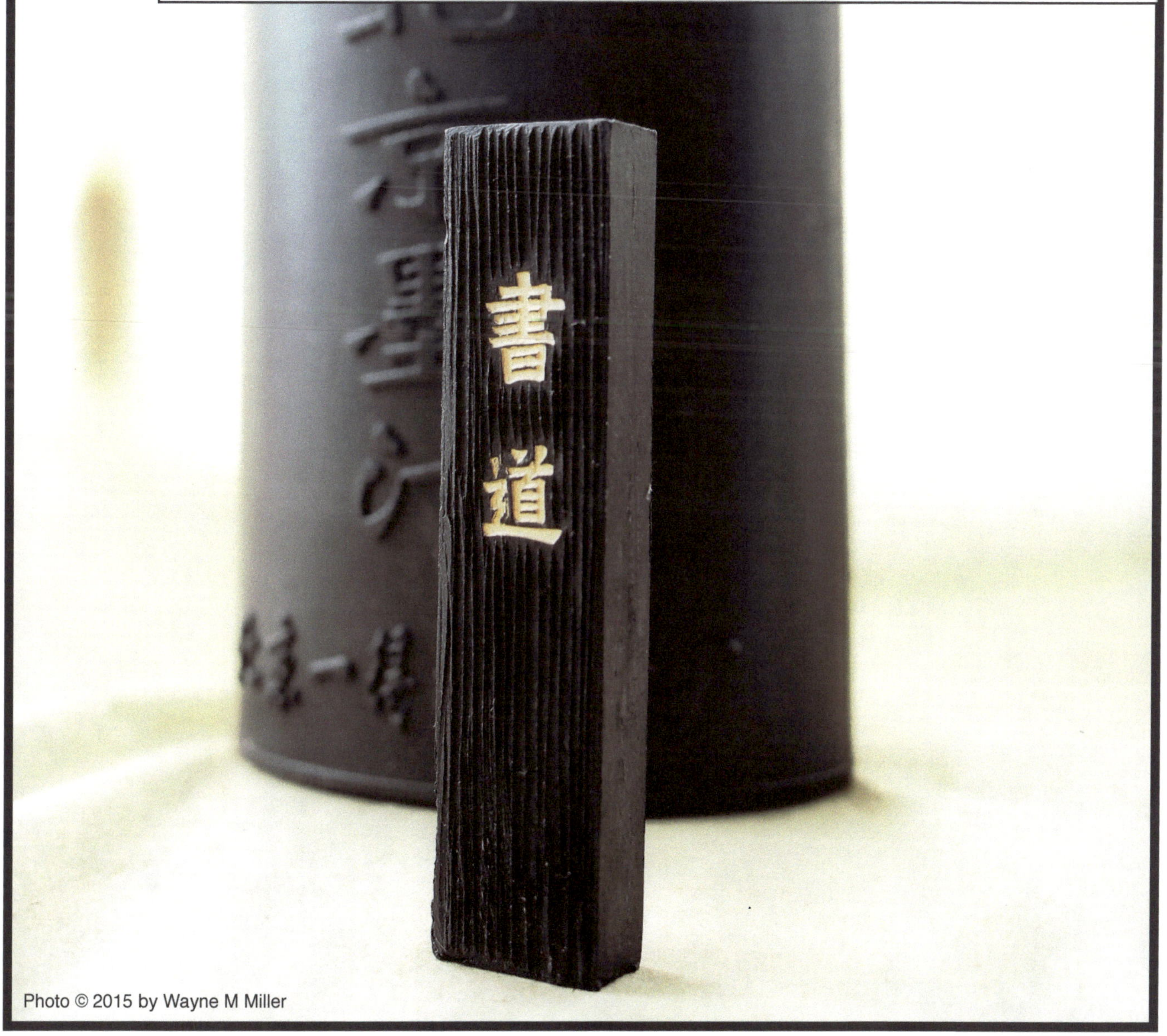

宣纸

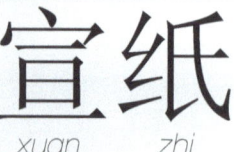

xuan   zhi

Silk was a common medium for painting and calligraphy in ancient China, it was cheaper than the expensive paper of the time. Now the reverse is true, therefore paper is almost exclusively used.

Modern production has made paper affordable, thus allowing artists access to its preferred characteristics. *Xuan zhi* is durable, strong, soft, and has a lightly textured surface.

There are two differint kinds to be noted:

Sheng Xuan: Absorbs water and ink, it is used for Chinese calligraphy and paintings in the *xieyi* style.

Shu Xuan: Does not absorb ink and is appropriate for the precise layout of paintings in *gongbi* style.

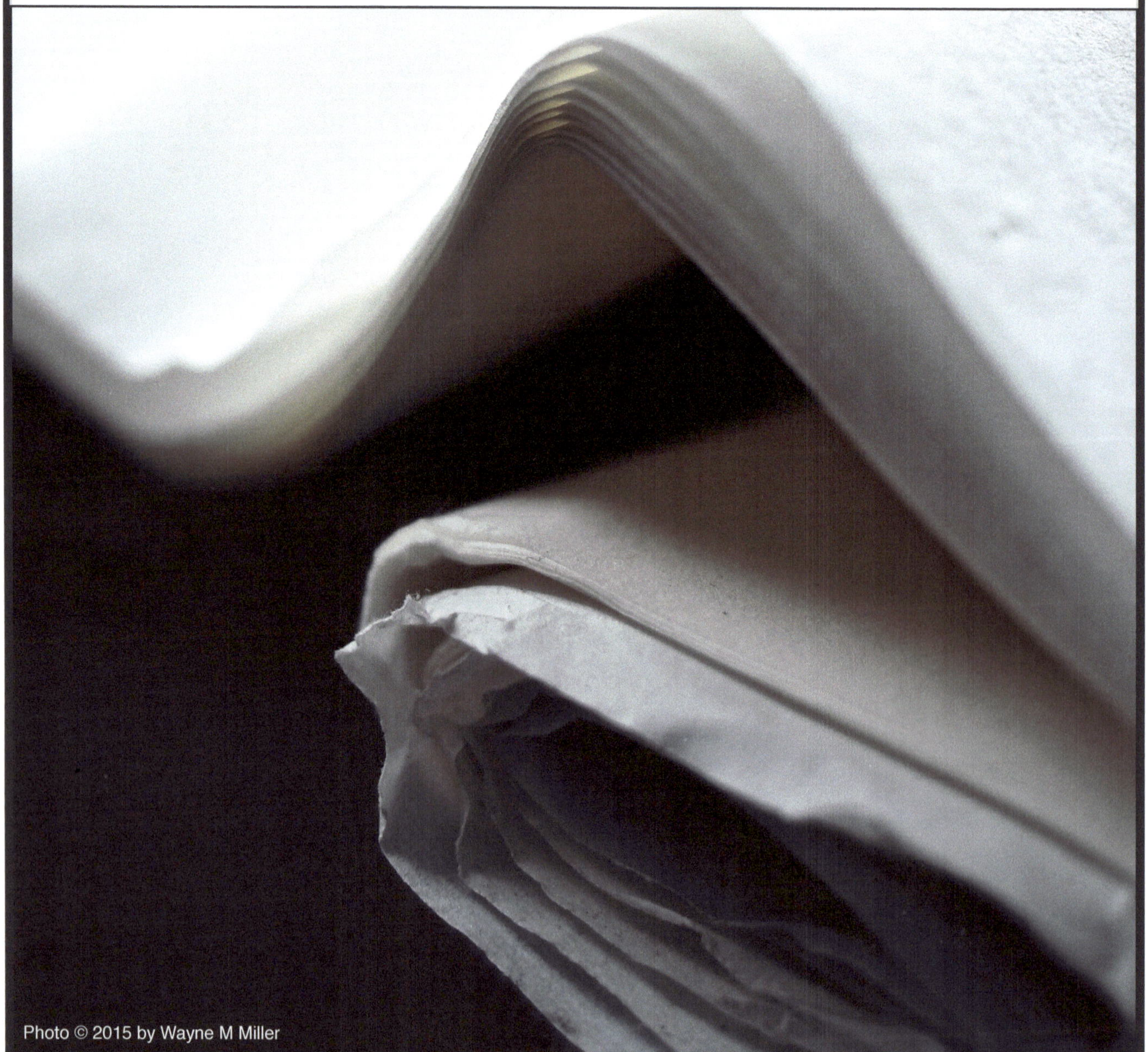

Photo © 2015 by Wayne M Miller

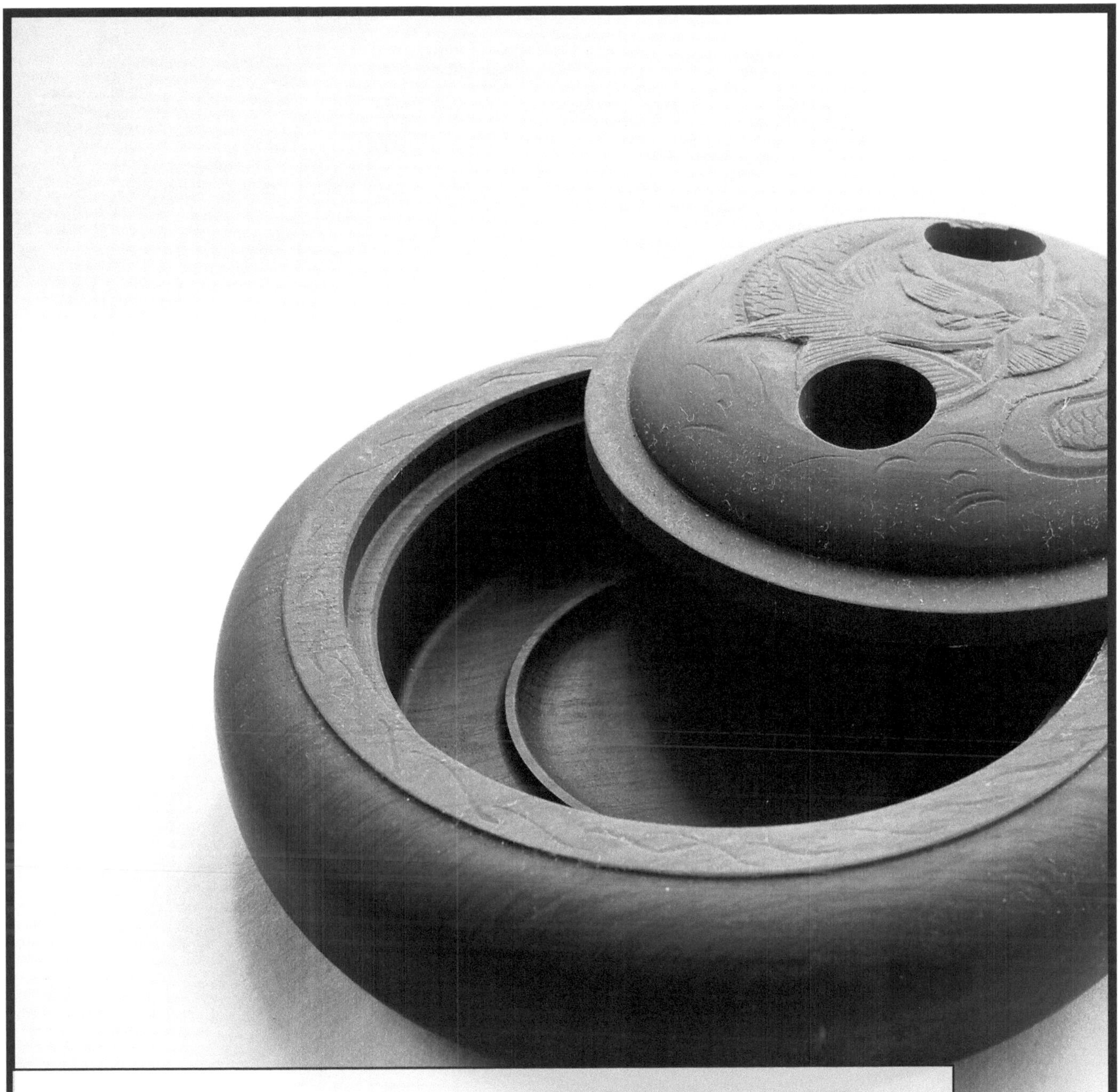

Inkwells or ink-stones are made of stone that has just the right consistency to grind the ink stick with water to form ink.

Grinding of the ink stick is done in a circular motion, adding water as needed until the desired consistency and shade is achieved.

Often the inkwell has a lid to cover the mix for in-between sessions, keeping the ink from drying out.

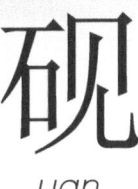

硯

yan

中国画

CHINESE PAINTING

Distinguishing features:

Common in quintessential monotone form, just raw ink and paper.

Color is typically conservative, often with a single hue to offset ink and paper.

Three main subjects: Animals, Landscapes and People.

Chinese painting is one of the oldest continuing artistic traditions in the world. To appreciate, one must first consider the viewing approach. For example, think of the first time you encountered an unfamiliar food, like a crab. Before you can enjoy the sweet meat of the crustacean, a strategy is required to get past its shell. The same can be said for appreciating Chinese art.

This strategy for appreciation is different from how you view western art that holds to the visual qualities of photography and the easily appreciated standards of composition, detail and color.

Traditional Chinese art requires a different standard. You must also consider culture, history and technique. Like watching a sport, the more you understand it, the more you enjoy it.

STRATEGY

Chinese art is all about

THE LINE

In calligraphy, every stroke forms a line that conveys meaning. The same can be said for painting, where mastering the stroke is the most important factor of painting.

The line refers to the quality and feel of these strokes.

When learning, one first practices the individual components, the smaller strokes, called radicals, as in the calligraphy below. After study, components are compiled, to make whole characters or an entire painting containing the appropriate components.

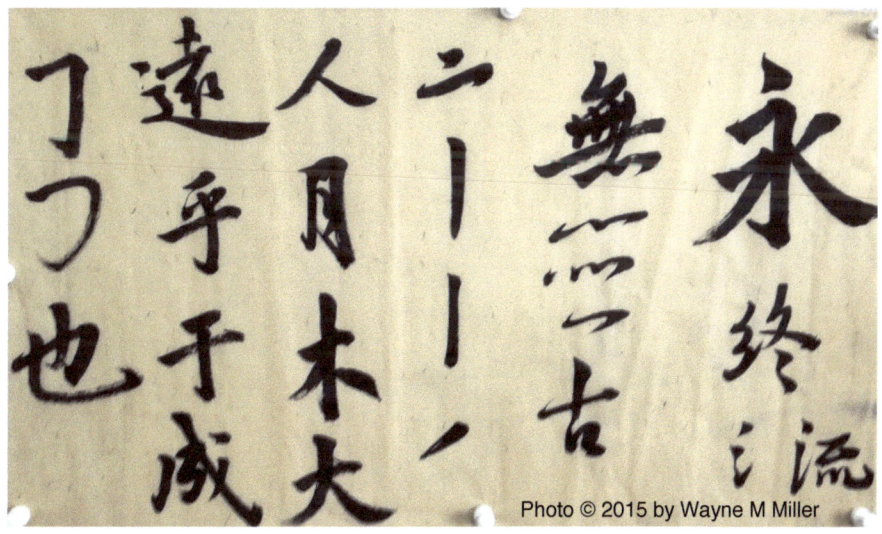

Photo © 2015 by Wayne M Miller

If you feel intimidated by the vast array of different forms and strokes, do not worry. Think of listening to songbirds in the trees, you don't have to know how they sing or what they are saying to sense their songs are good. Just enjoy the form and feeling.

For Starters: Familiarize yourself with the two basic painting styles, Meticulous and Abstract.

11

STYLES

Meticulous

工笔
gong   *bi*

The "*gong*" character means work, while "*bi*" means brush.
High detail, fine coloration, and life-like subjects characterize this working brush style.
Commonly one piece takes months or years to complete. *Gongbi* is the oldest form of traditional Chinese painting.

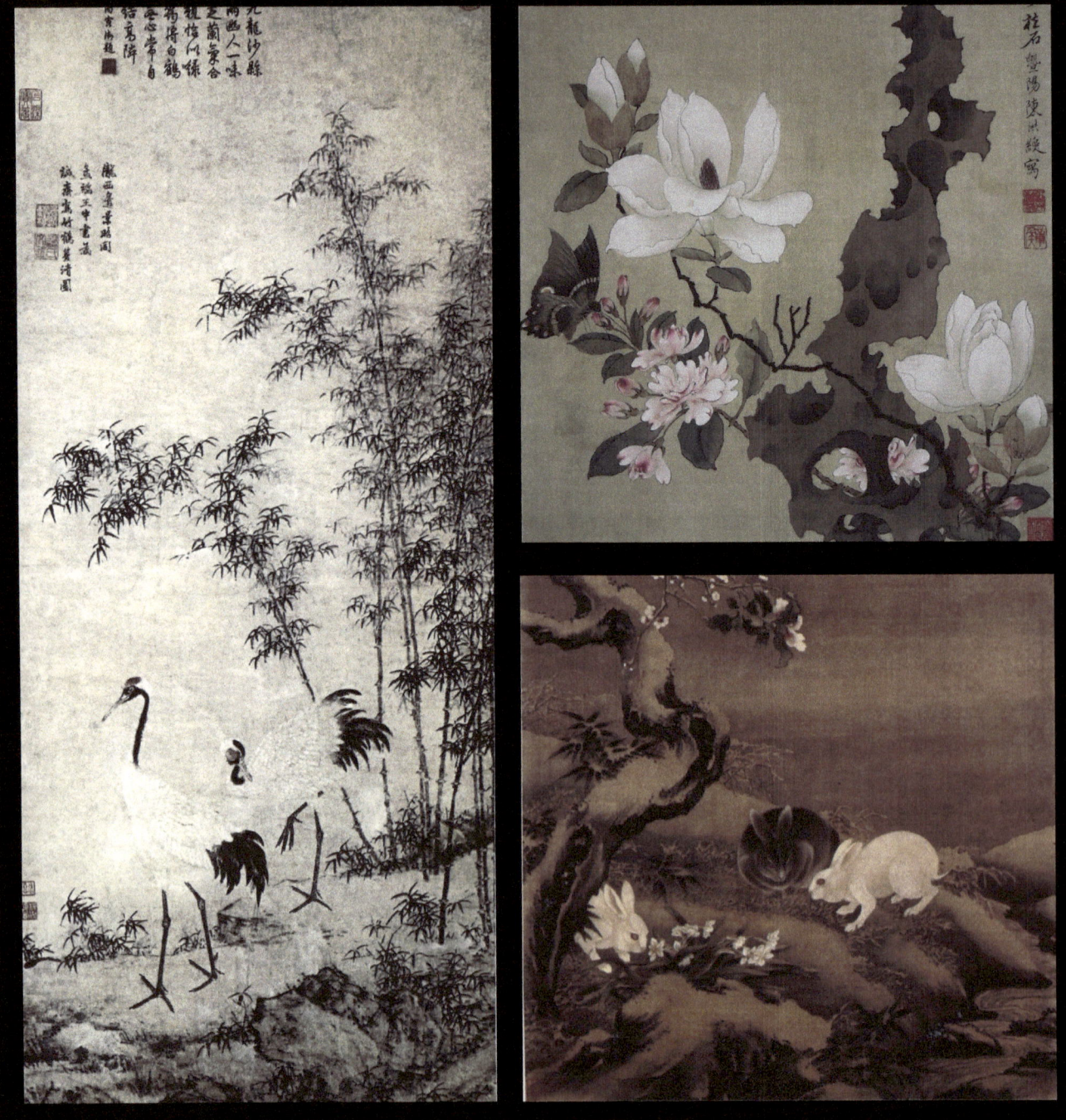

STYLES

Abstract

写意
xia   *yi*

"*Xia*" means, to write or sketch, while the character "*yi*" means idea or thought. Together *xiayi* means "sketching one's thoughts".

Expressive and freeform, *xiayi* is the most abstract of traditional Chinese painting. Often appearing deceptively simple in comparison to *gongbi,* in reality *xiayi* is the most difficult style to master.

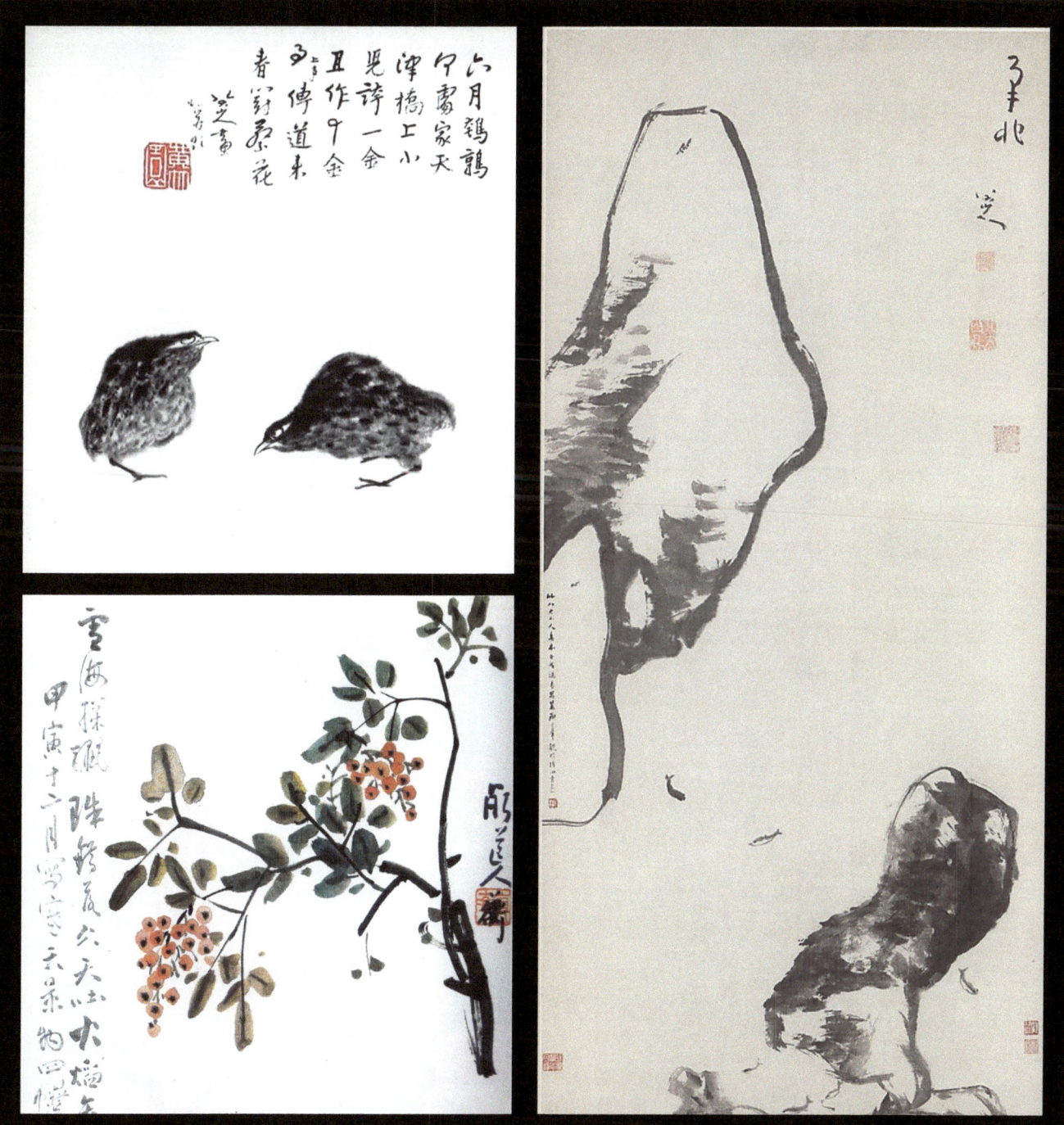

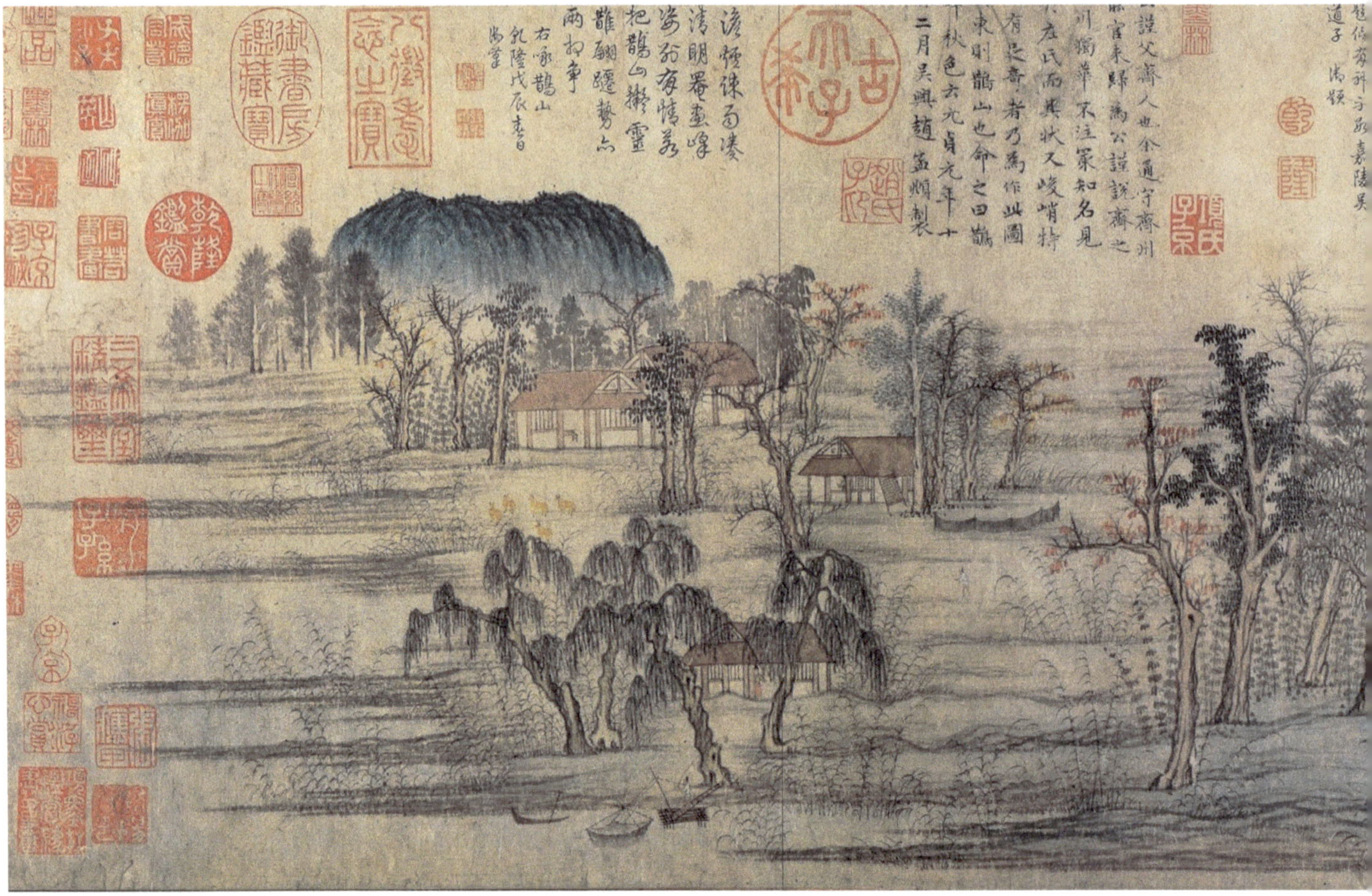

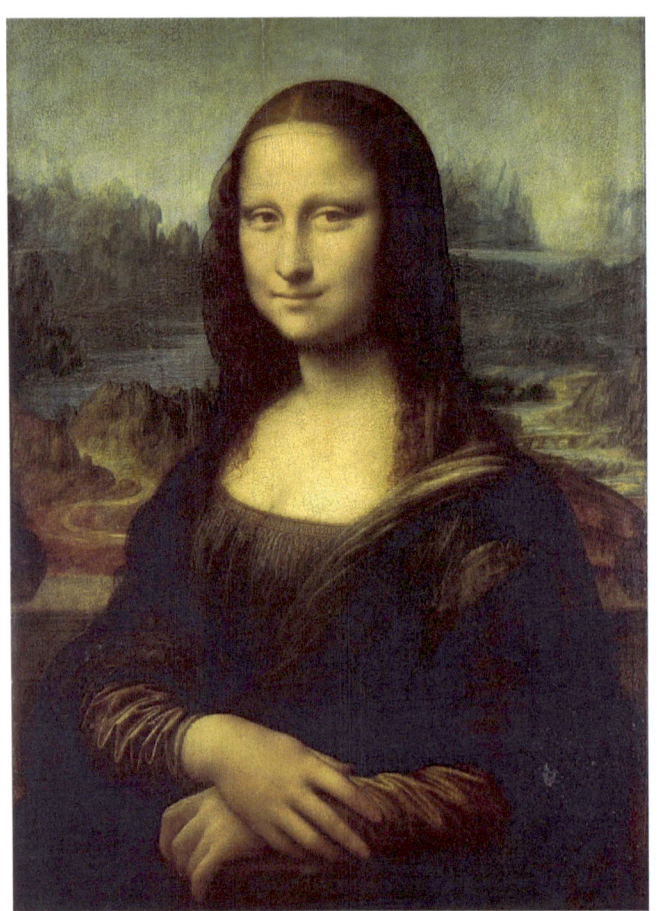

FAME

VS *Chinese Art*
Western Art

What makes a painting great?
Chinese paintings are not very famous compared to iconic pieces of western art. Why is this?

In general, people pay more attention to western art. Also, because of the country's socialist bend, students in Chinese schools are often shown art from political leaders instead of good artists.

Thus, young aspiring Chinese artists copy western art instead of the rich history of art they already have. Perhaps this explains why the history of Chinese art remains obscure in modern times.

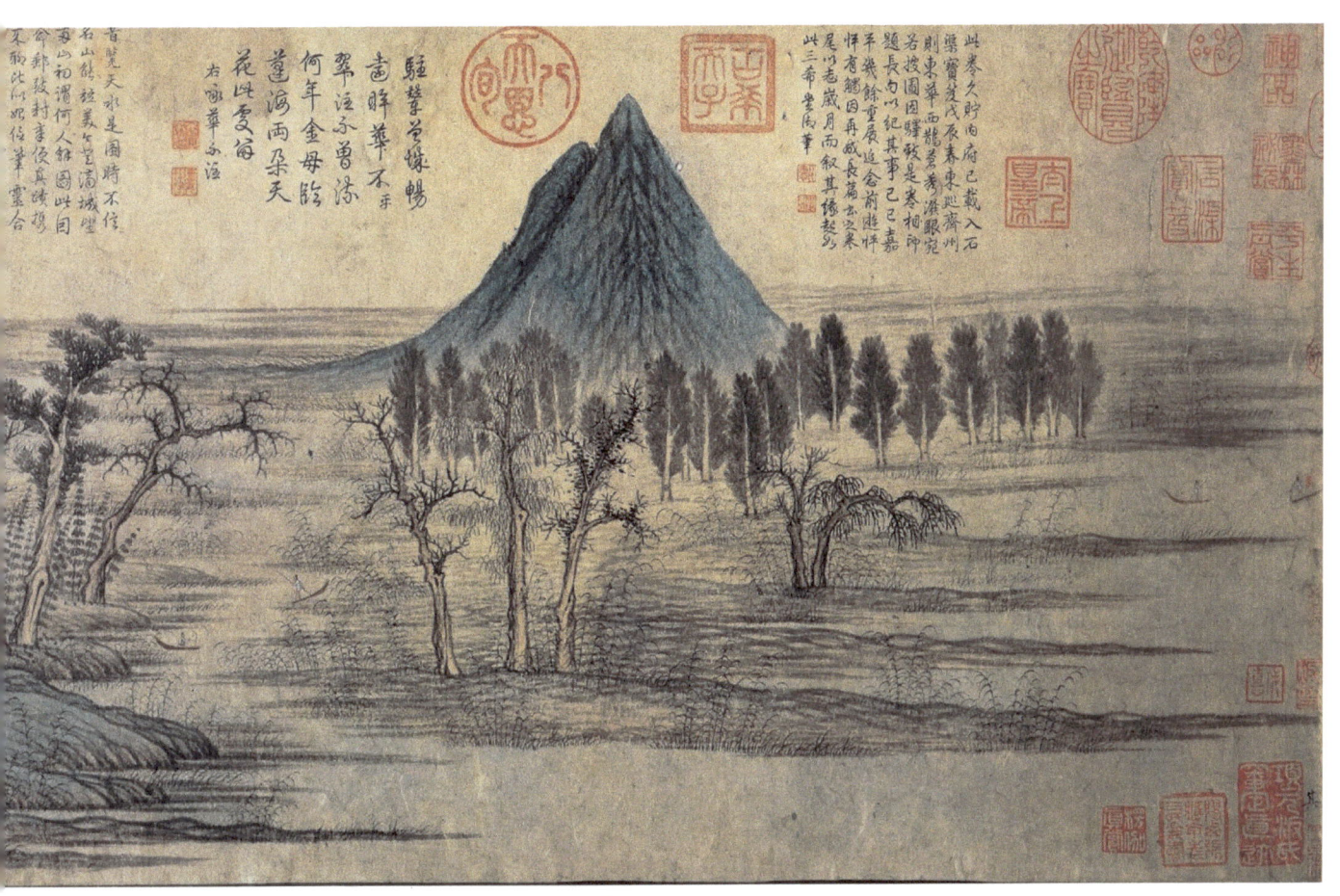

I invite you to examine two masterpieces and discover striking similarities.
At left, *Mona Lisa*, the famous portrait. All can appreciate the three-dimensional aspects of the picture. Beyond her iconic face, the road, mountains, sky and water invite your eyes to linger. Painted around 1503 AD. Its perspective is momentous in art history.

Now turn your attention above to *Autumn Colors on the Qiao and Hua Mountains* painted by *Zhao Mengfu* (赵孟頫) in 1295 AD, over two hundred years before *Mona*. The painting carries a similar feeling of great distance. Detail in the trees and boats construct a unique and equally impressive three-dimensional perspective.

In addition to this mastery of perspective, the use of two mountains is usually hard to balance and yet, the equilibrium achieved with the pair of mountains is the painting's distinguishing characteristic. Also similar to the blank space left for *Mona's* sky, blank space is used here to convey water in a lake.

Less noticeable to the casual observer is the line of the painting, the brushwork that takes years of study and practice to understand. This defining trait may well be the same thing that keeps this and other Chinese art from the fame of its western counterparts.

Unlike western art with its accessible standards, traditional Chinese art is bound by its unique yet slightly egotistic styles, rules and strategies that can deter the subject from gaining popularity beyond its own clique. That being said, to join in the study of this topic is to enjoy one of the oldest continuing artistic traditions in the world, where the rewards are beautiful and unique.

LANDSCAPES
Mountain and Water

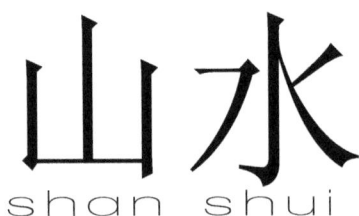

shan shui

Shan shui is typically the most highly regarded style of Chinese painting. Often large, covering a whole wall, one first views from a distance to admire the size and composition, then steps closer to examine the fine detail.

Appreciation tips:
Shan shui is not meant to replicate the appearance of nature but rather capture the essence and emotion in the rhythm of nature.

Look for the source of water and where it flows.
Look for a path. If one exists, it should lead somewhere.
Look for buildings or boats and how to get to them.

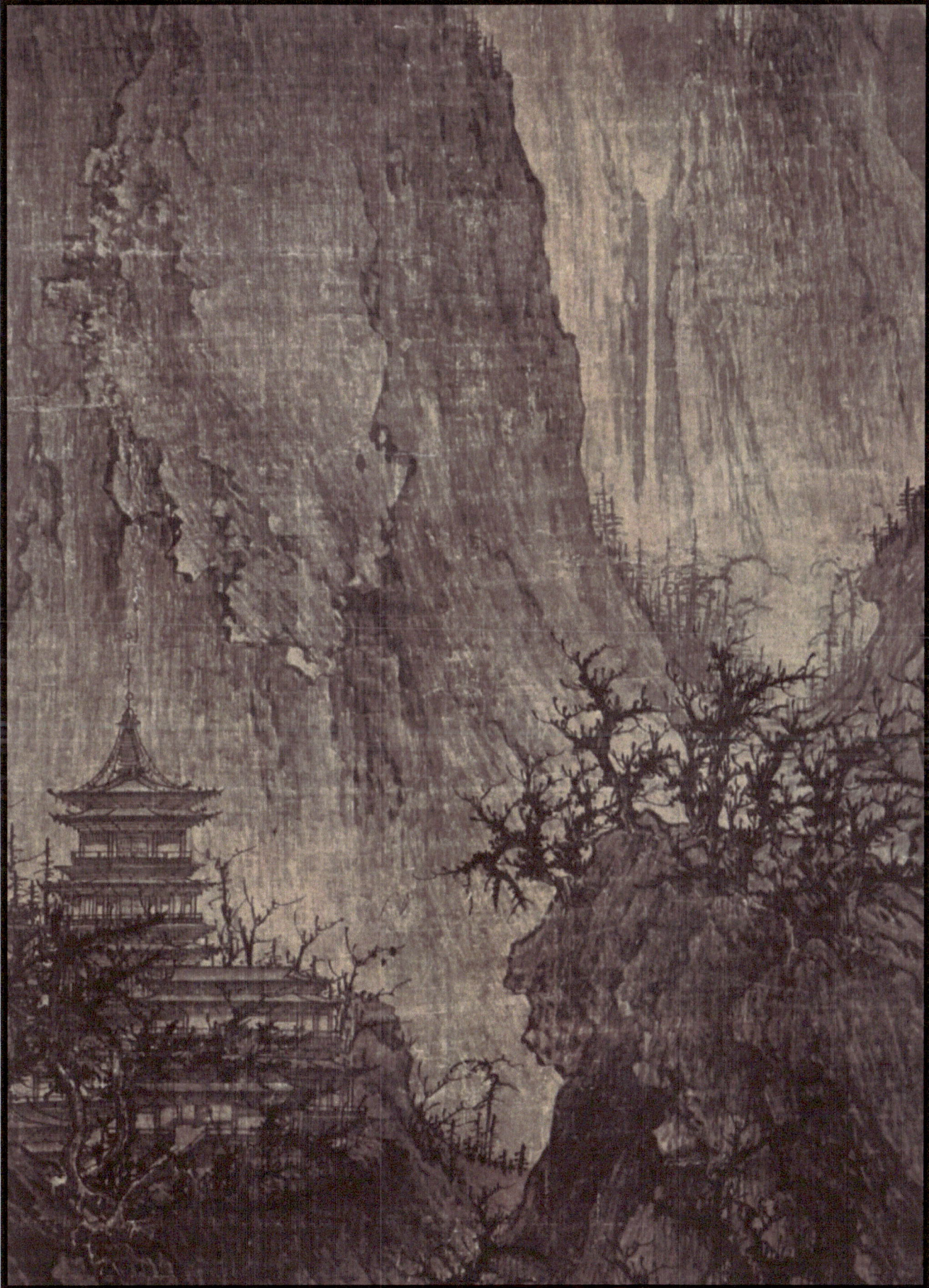

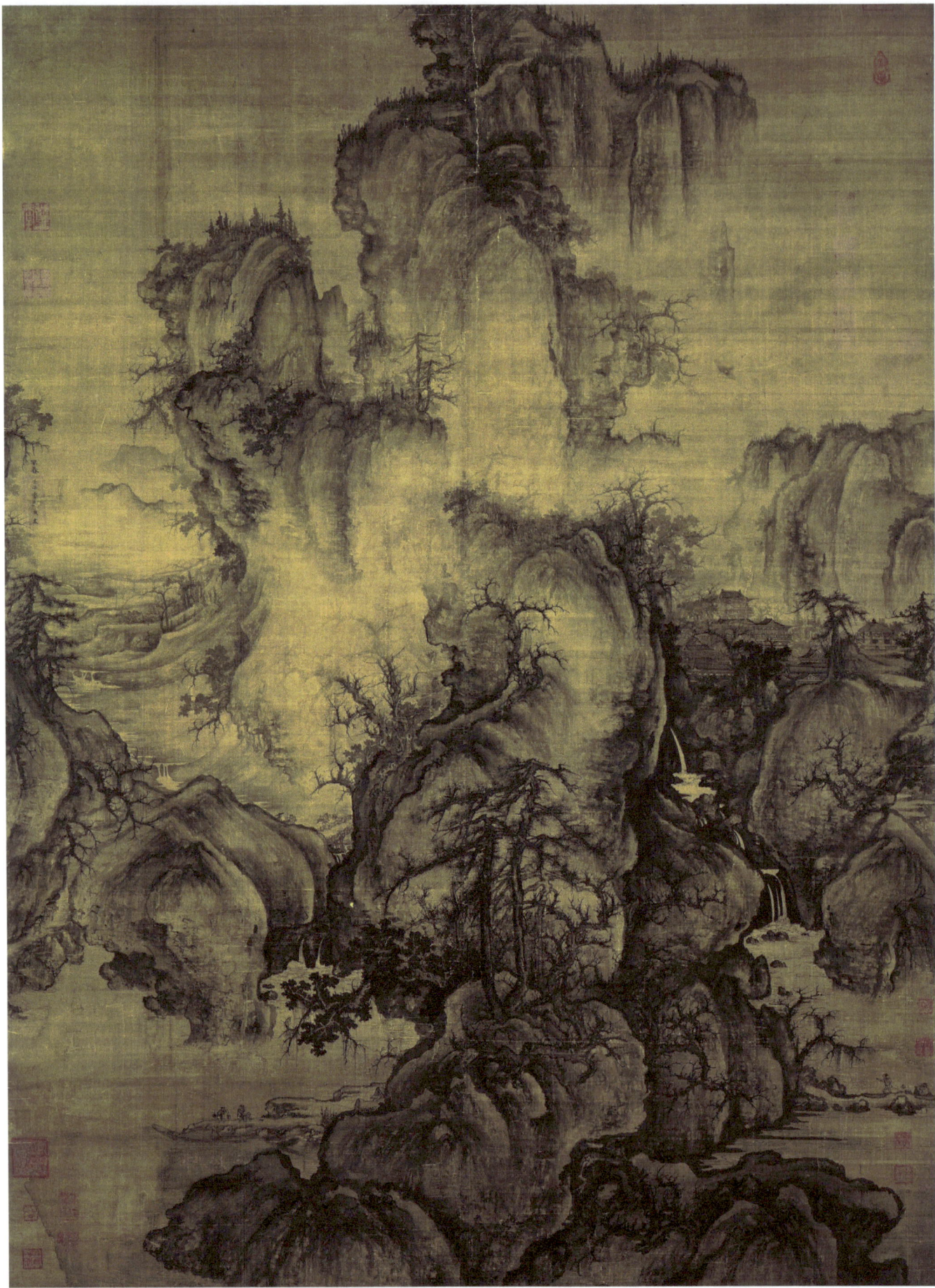

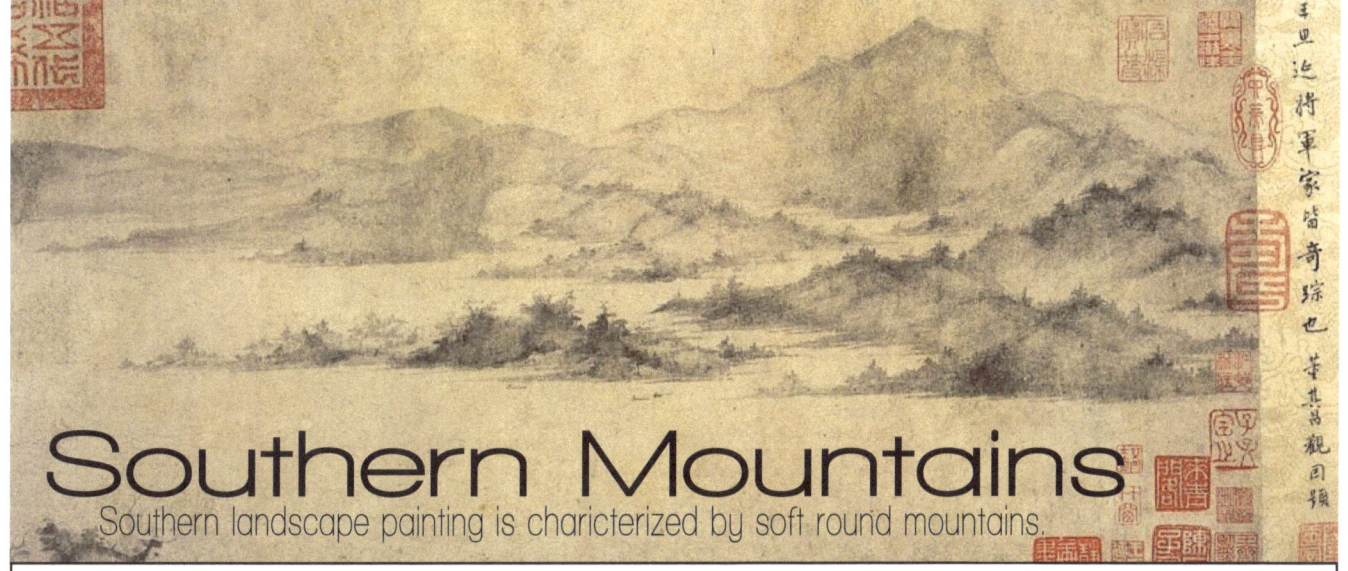

Southern Mountains

Southern landscape painting is charicterized by soft round mountains.

Above: Minimalist mountains may at first appear as shadows, but a closer look will reval finely detailed brushwork, conveying forest, trees and water. Painted in the12th century by Li Shi (李氏) Titled: *Imaginary Tour Through Xiao-xiang*.

Left: *Early Spring* by Guo Xi 1072 AD. A masterpice of 山水. Notice the depth of perspective, detail, and perfect use of contrast for composition. To the left of center you see a valley with houses, while lower down, at the waters edge, are boats and people.

Below: *Dwelling in the Fuchun Mountains*, Huang Gongwang (1269–1354). A small surviving piece of a long scroll is renowned for its expertly placed brush strokes. It displays very typical southern style, a soft sweeping landscape.

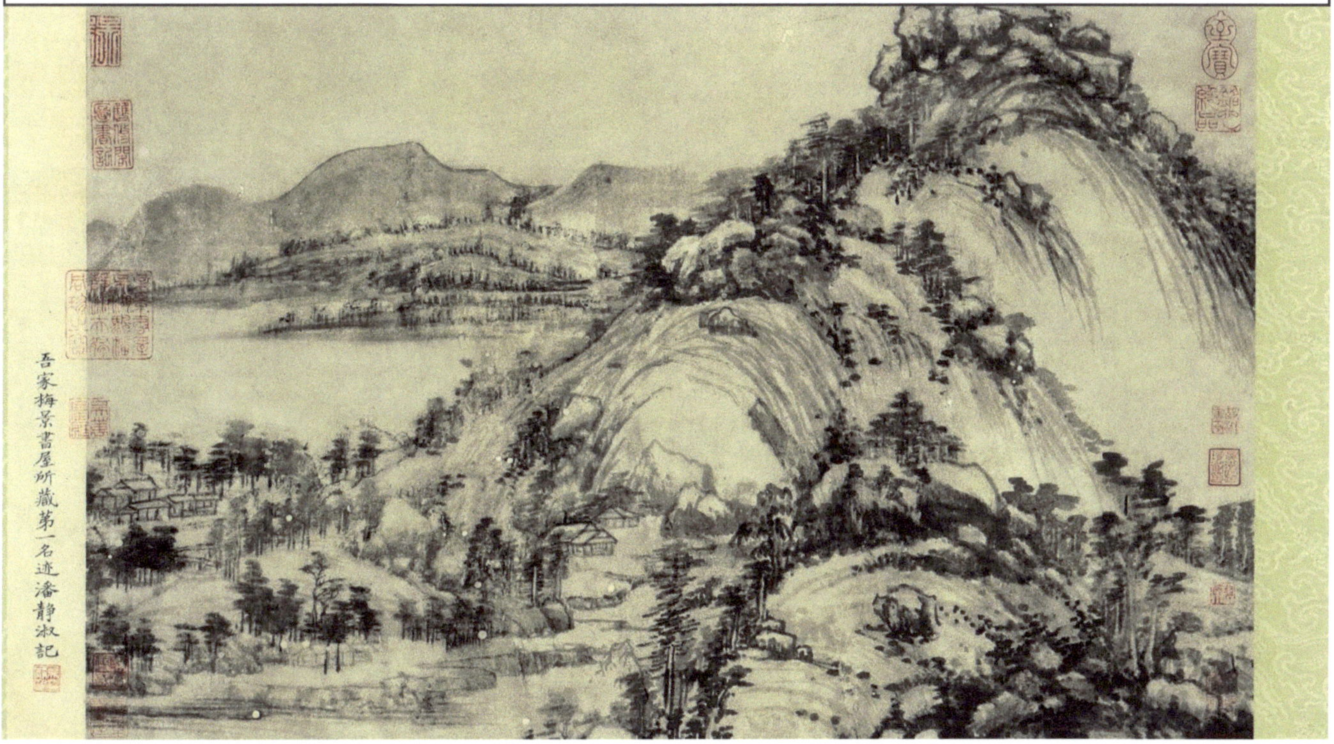

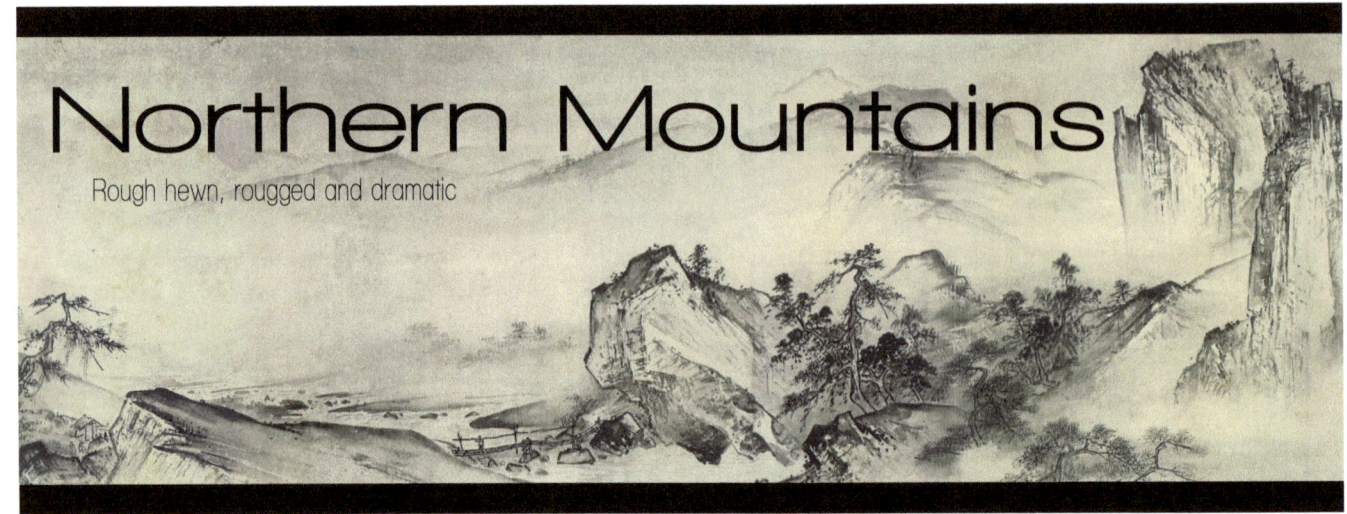

Northern Mountains

Rough hewn, rougged and dramatic

Top and Bottom: *In Clear View of Streams and Mountains*. By Xia Gui (夏圭) 13th century. A fine example of Northern Mountains which look jagged and rough, as if hewn by an axe. Compare this to the soft "Southern Mountains" displayed previously. This is a regional difference of painting style.

Common to both is the use of blank space to covey the expression of mist and water.

Right: *Dancing and Singing Peasants Returning from Work*, By Ma Yuan (馬遠) 1160-1225 AD

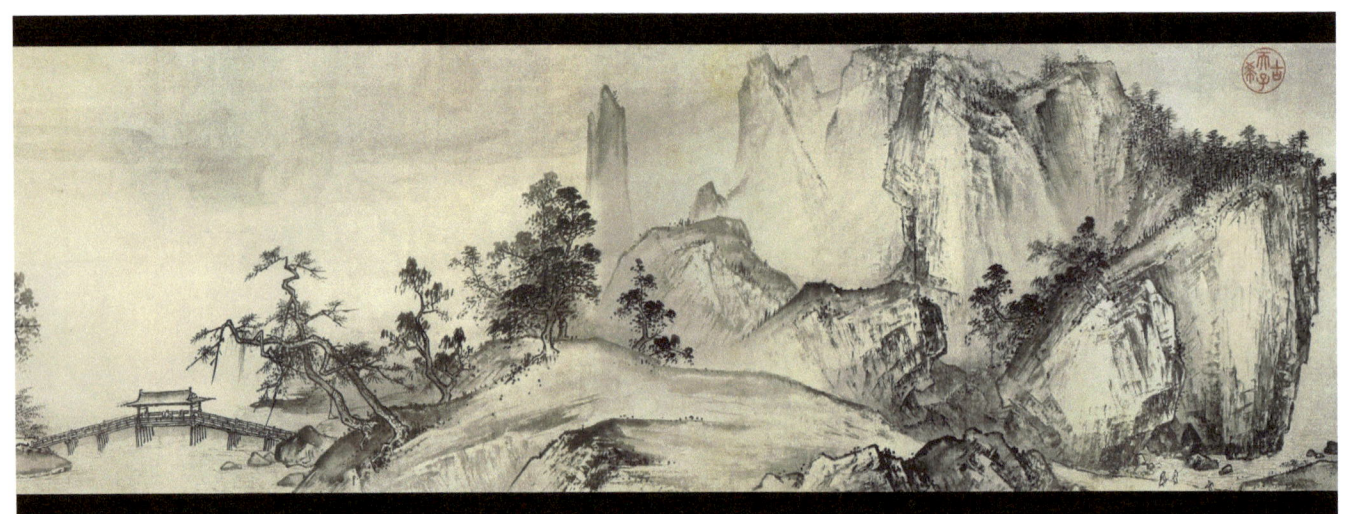

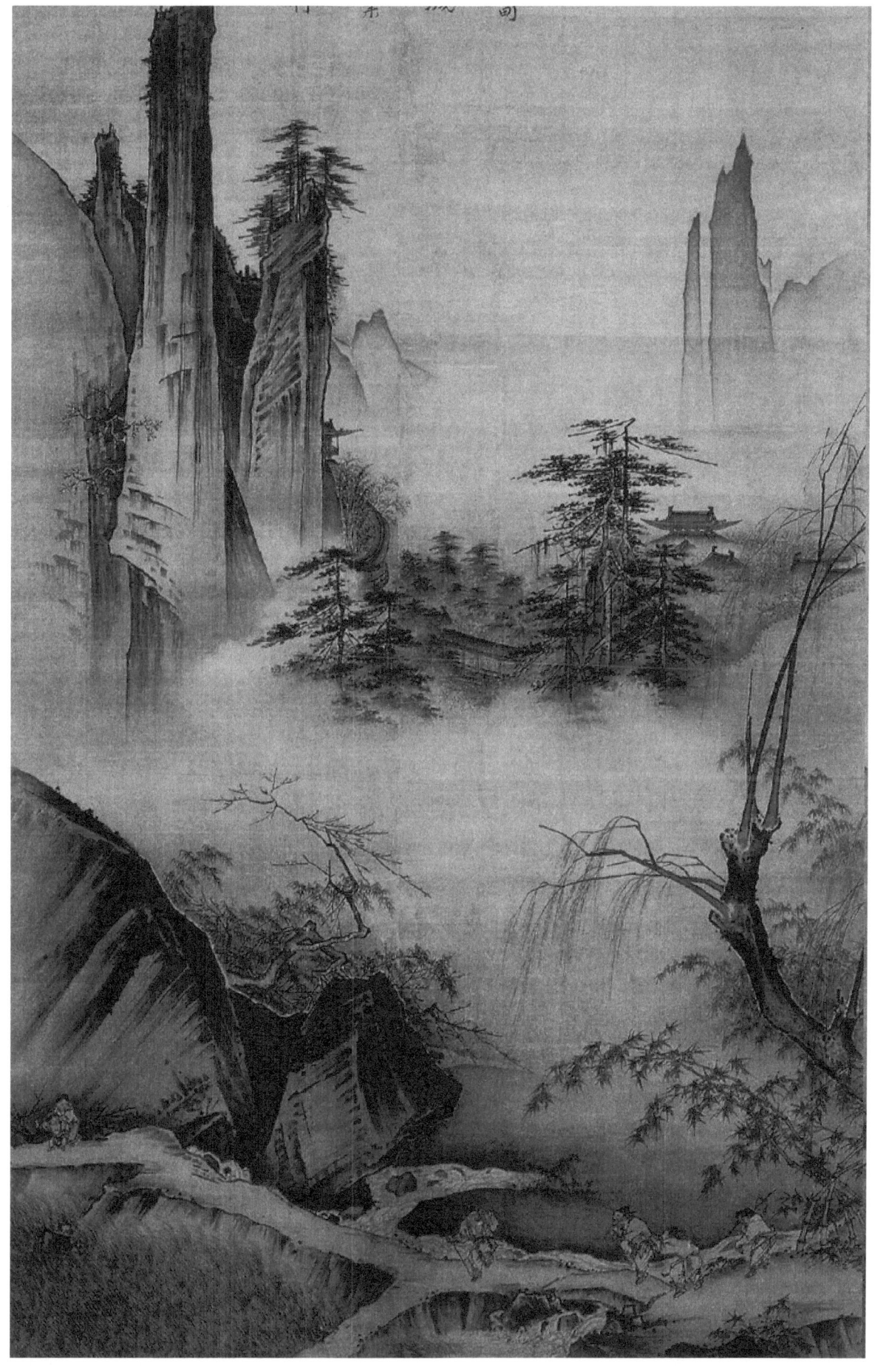

21

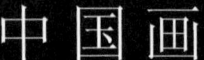

STYLES

BIRD & FLOWER
Plants and Animals

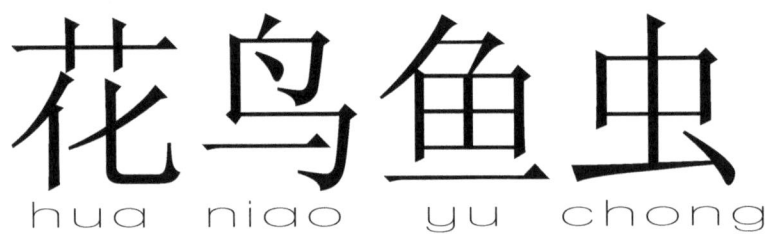

hua niao yu chong

Literally translated: Flower, Bird, Fish, Bug.

This form of traditional painting encompasses the whole natural world, typically isolating a subject in portrait form.

Appreciation tips:
In the *gongbi* style, centuries of development have standardized many subjects. Even poses are systemized and followed. Yet there is a large margin of expression, especially as one masters the forms of various subjects and develops their own unique form of brush strokes.

Many artists specialize in a single subject, such as bamboo, horses or tigers.

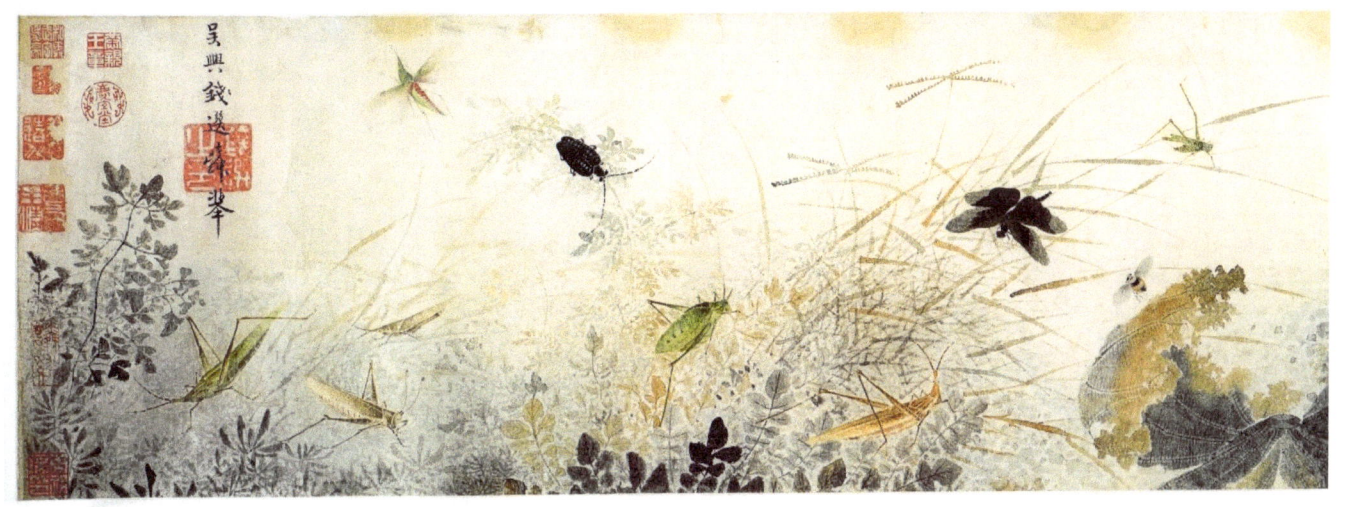

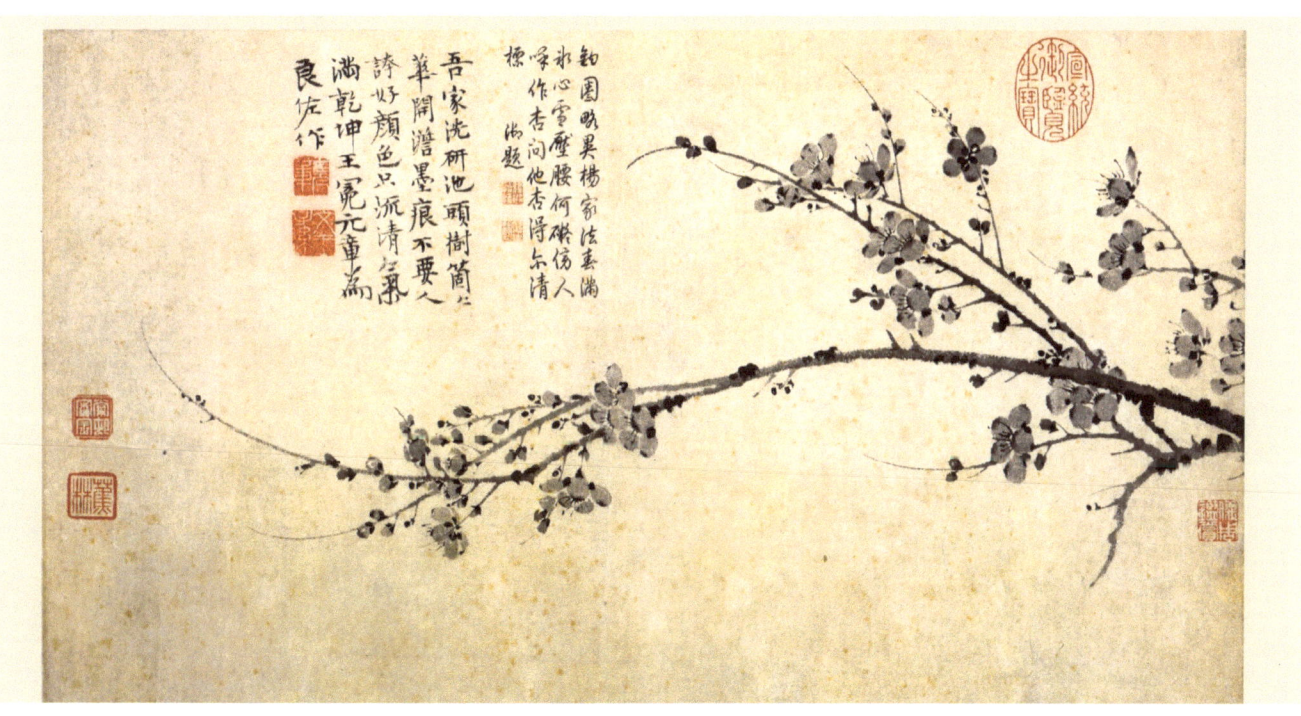

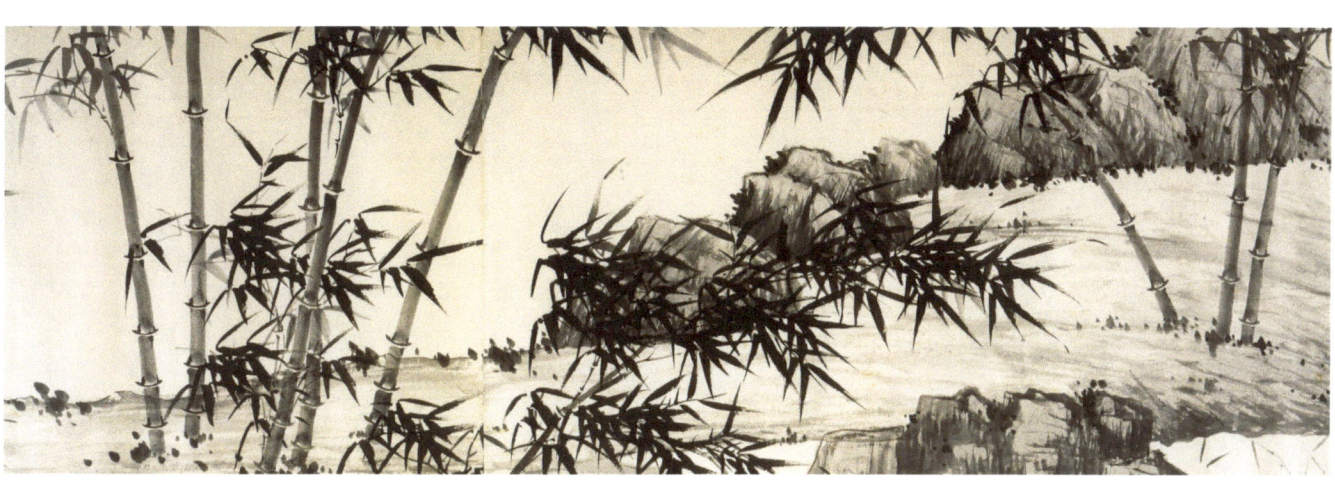

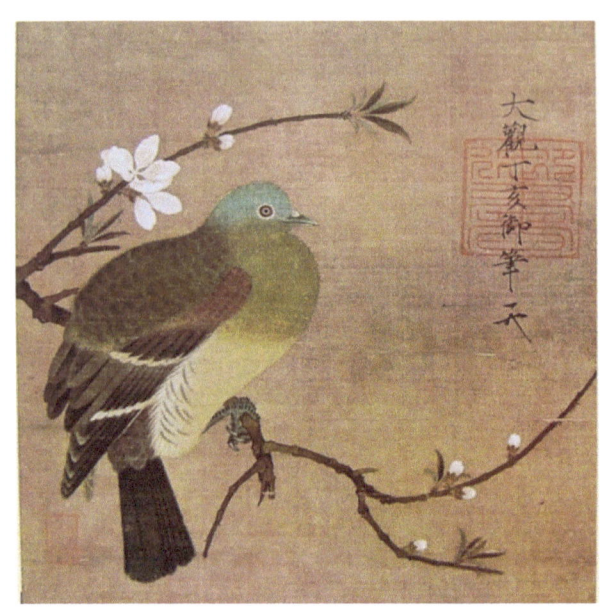

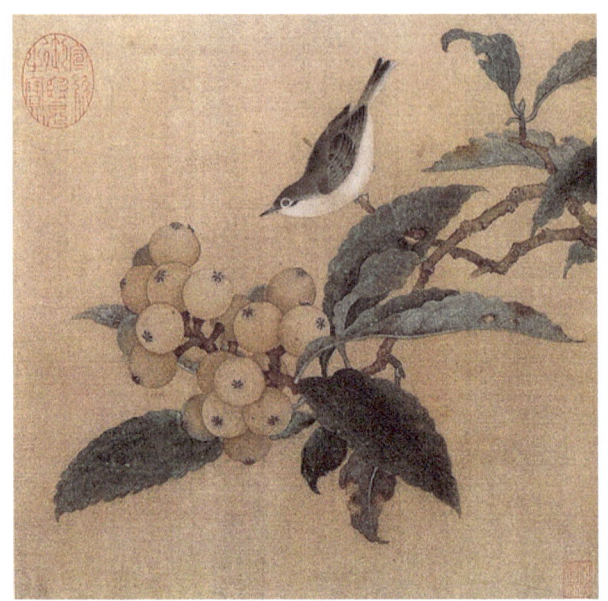

工笔
gong *bi*

Birds- METICULOUS

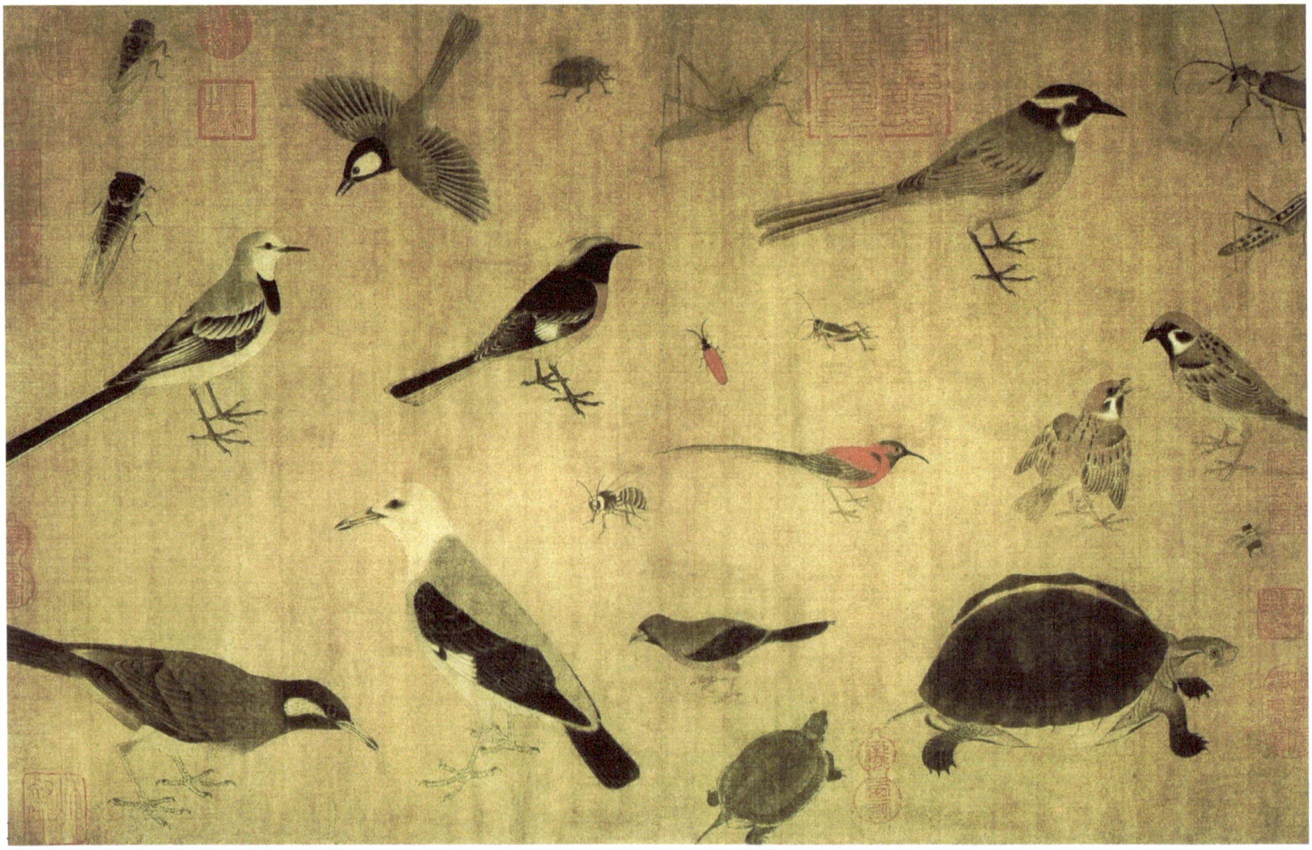

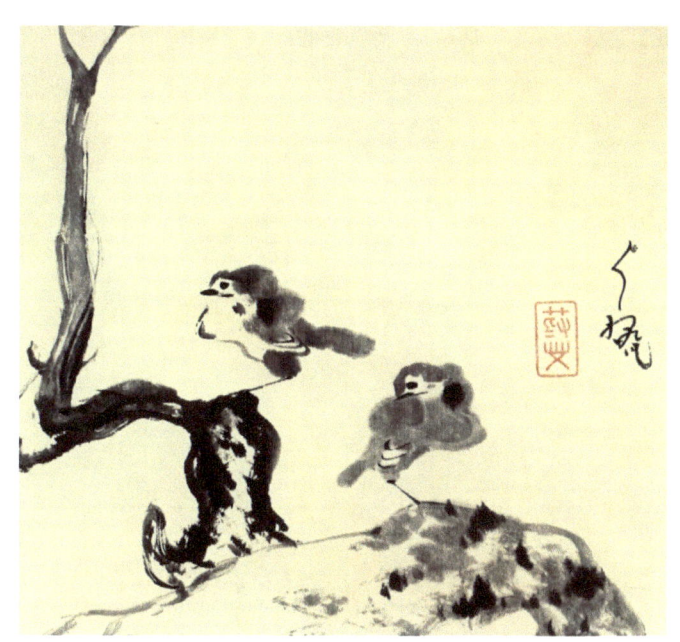

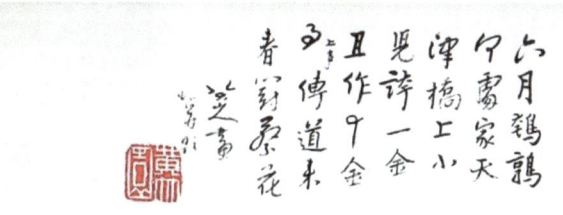

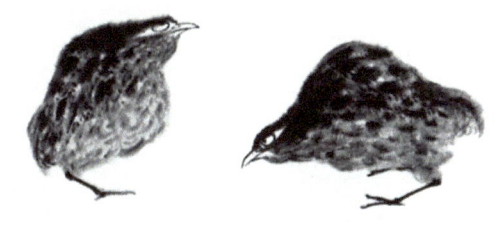

写意 Birds- ABSTRACT

xia yi

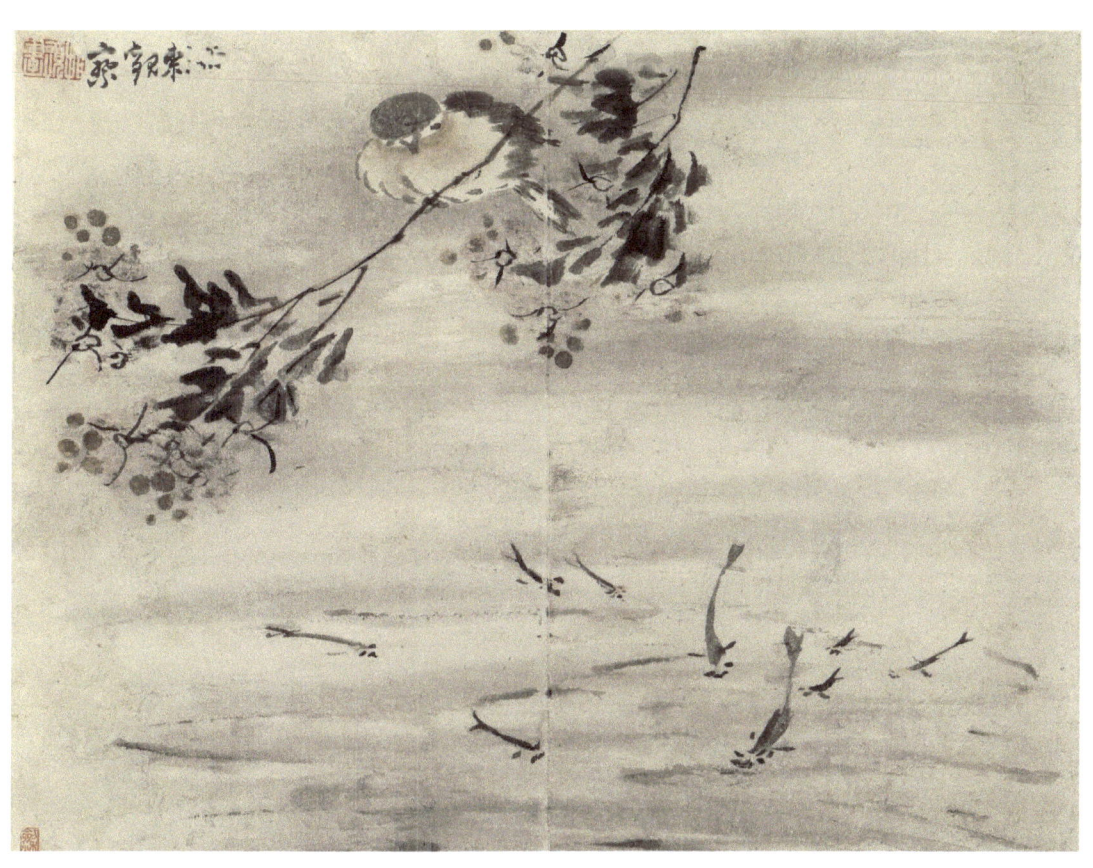

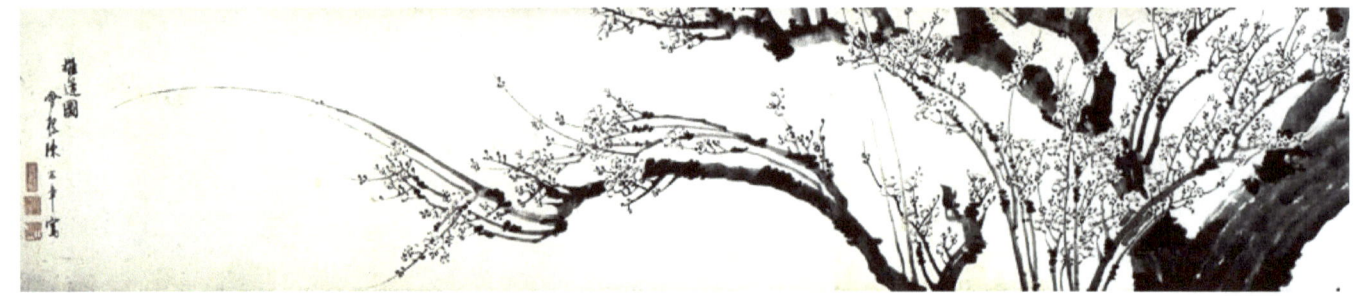

METICULOUS

Gongbi Style Flowers

工笔

gong *bi*

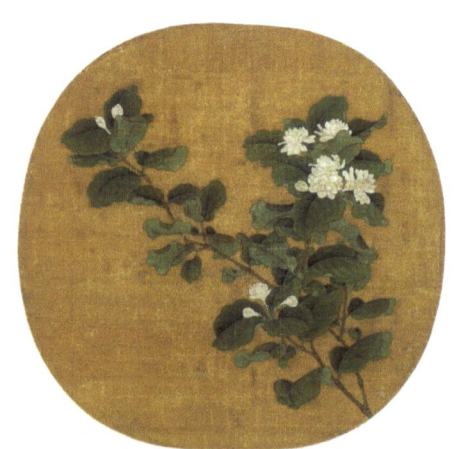

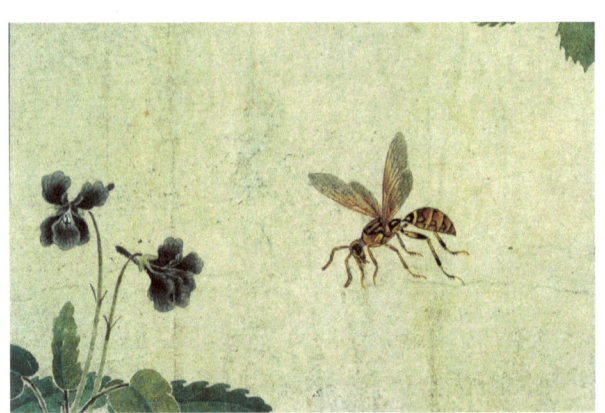

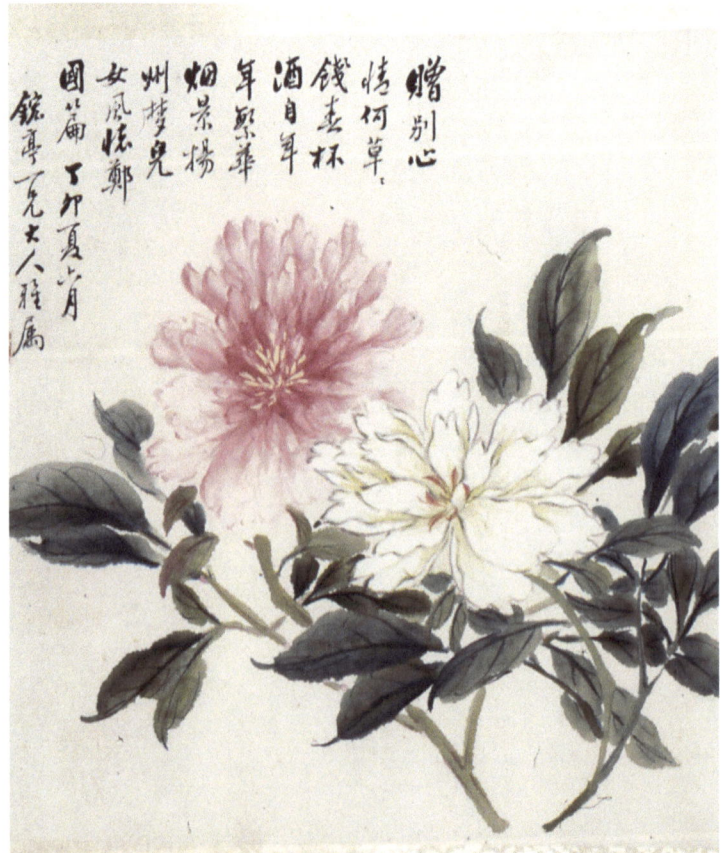

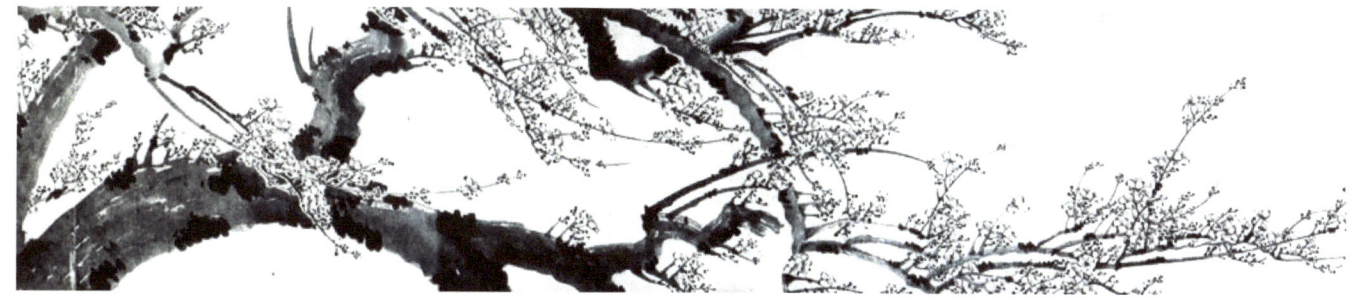

ABSTRACT

Xiayi Style Flowers

写意
xia　*yi*

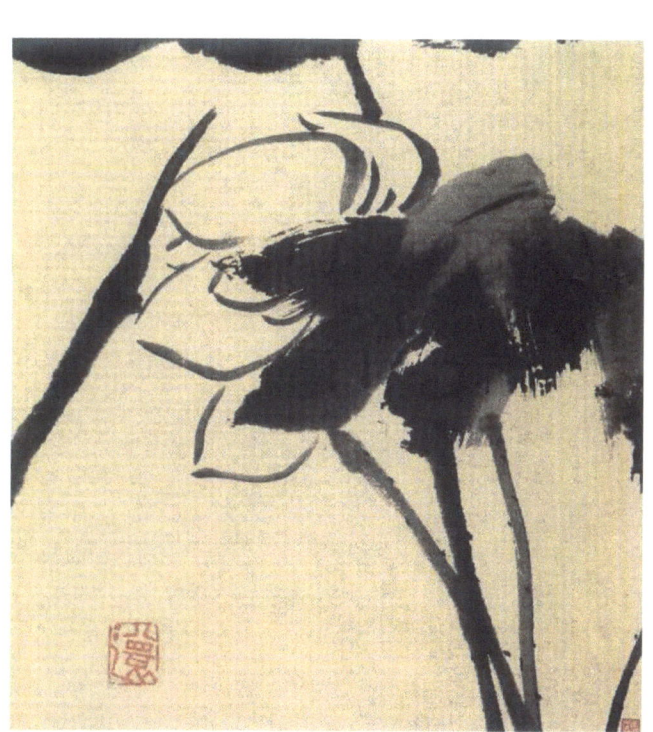

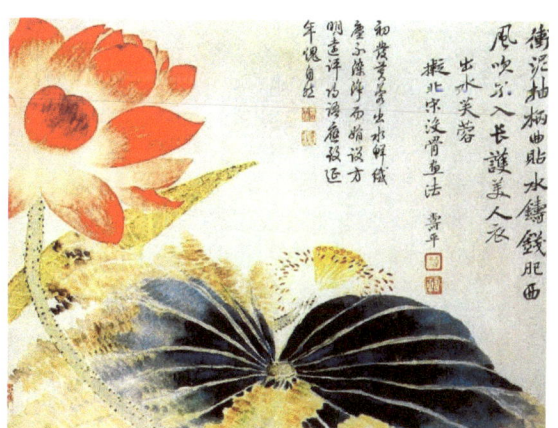

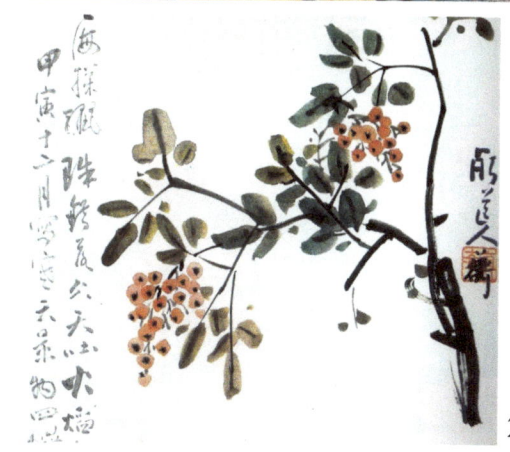

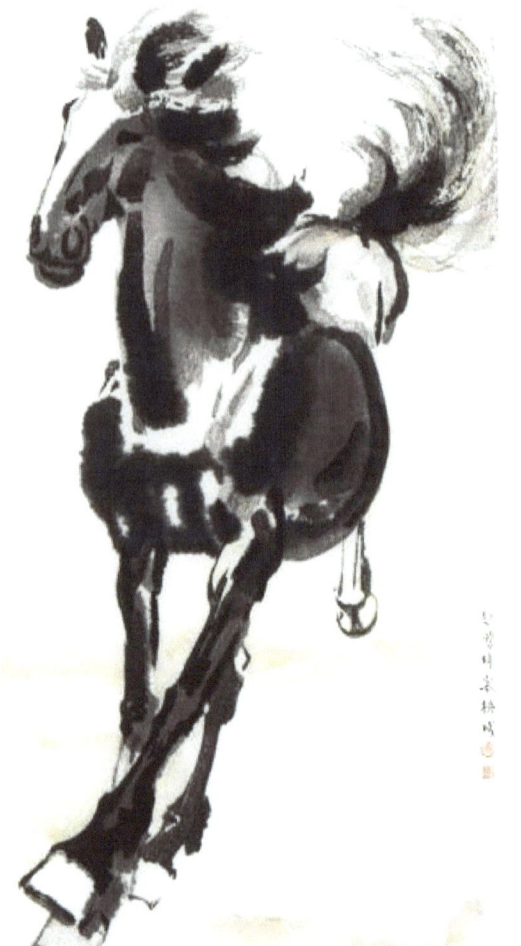

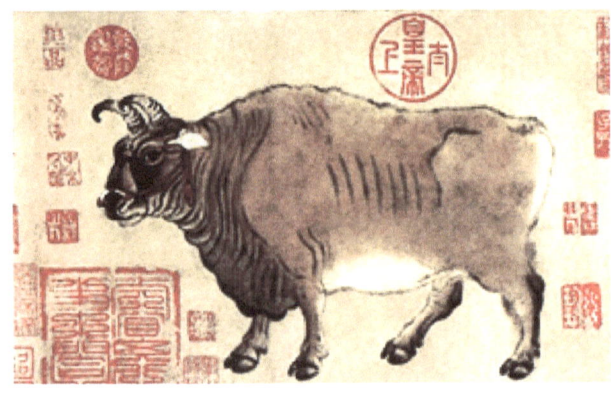

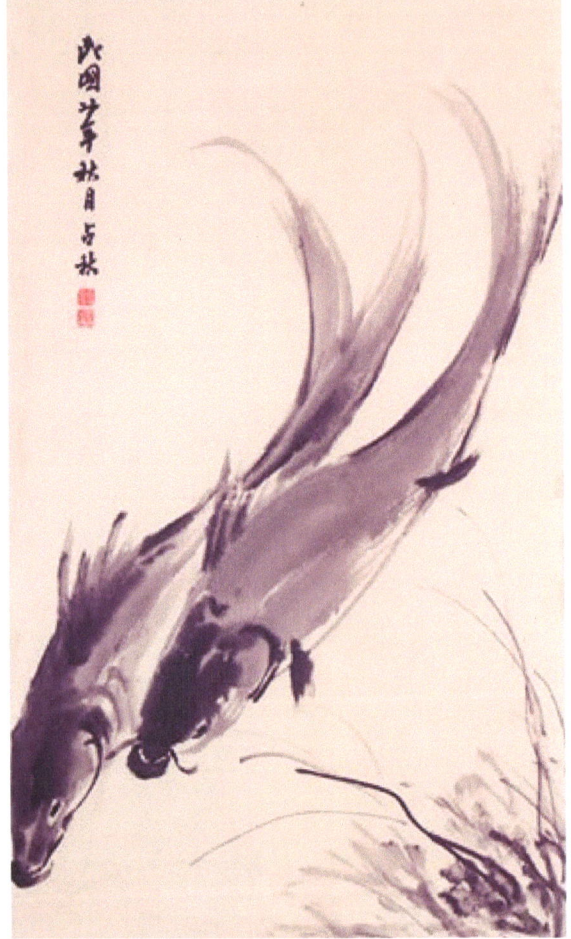

ANIMALS

Bird and flower style refers to all the animal kingdom: flora, fauna and scenes from nature. Here you see a *xiayi* horse, shrimp, some fish and a *gongbi* cow and goats.

Pay attention and sometimes you will see a mix of *gongbi* on *xiayi* styles within a painting.

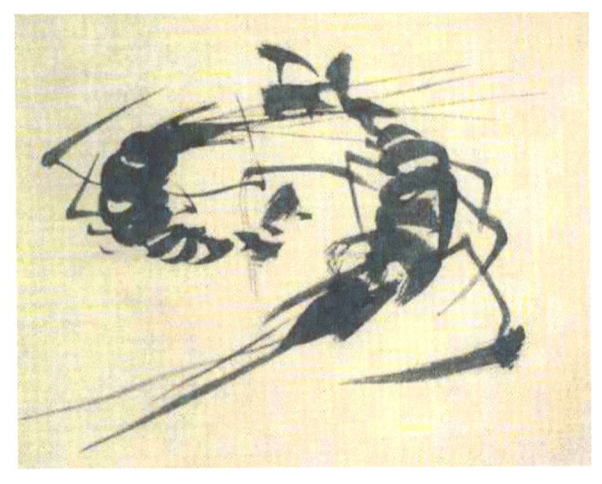

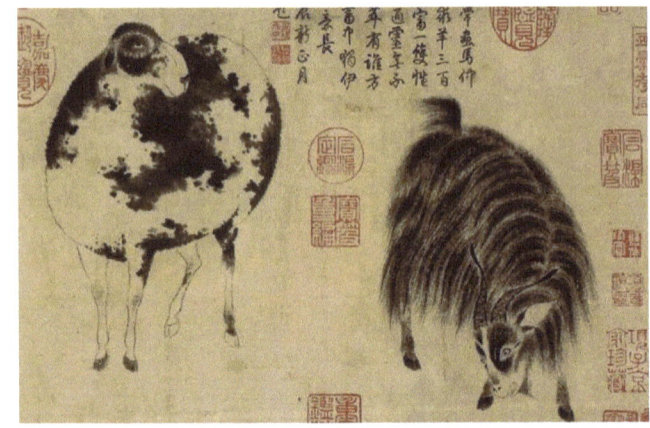

竹 *zhu-* BAMBOO

There is a deep connection between culture, characters and bamboo. For example, even the leaves have proper forms and often reflect the form and feeling of penmanship in the character *zhu*-the written Chinese form of bamboo.

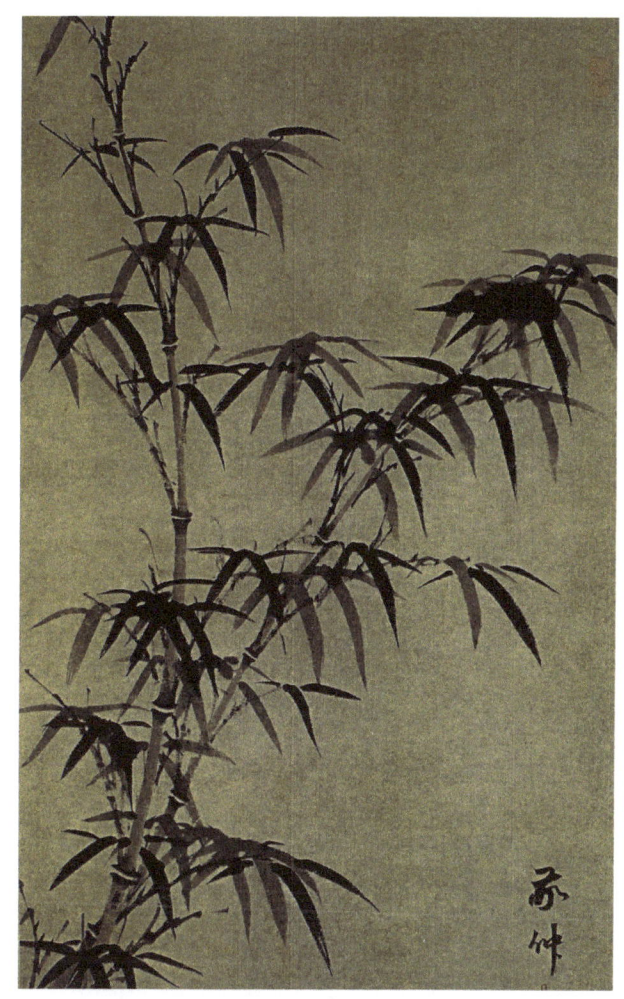

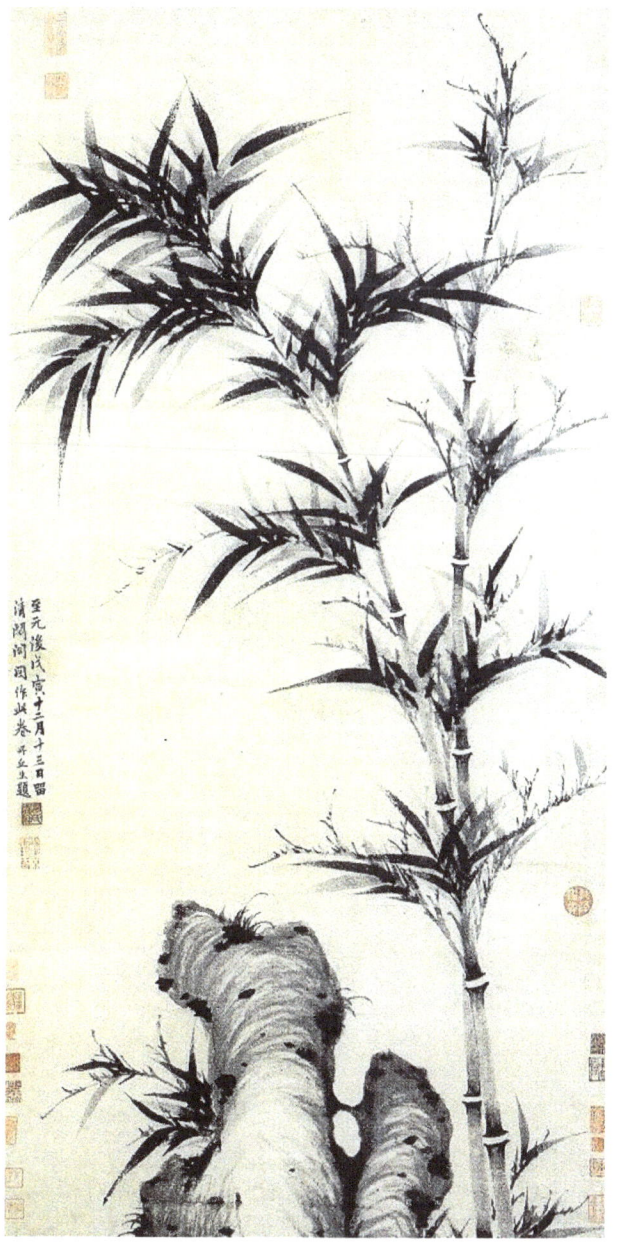

Honorable member of the bird and flower style, bamboo is regarded with virtues of humbleness, strength and resilience.

Specialized artists known as bamboo painters, devote their creative energy and practice solely to this subject.

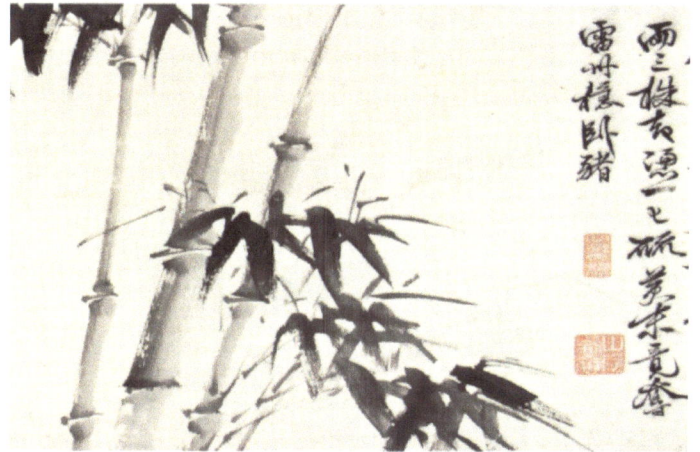

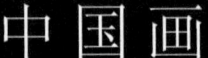

STYLES

PORTRAITURE
Figures and People

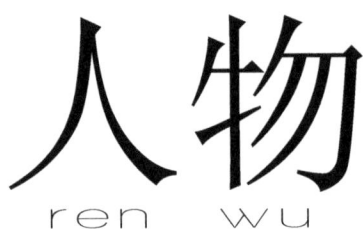

人物

ren   wu

Chinese portraiture originates from the ancient imperial court.
It was used to record court life and prominent people, much like
historical portraiture in western art.

Appreciation tips:
Strange clothing styles in a foreign environment can make it difficult to relate with these paintings. Yet even to the modern viewer,
they contain a unique perspective and emotion.

Subjects traditionally painted reflect dignity and a regal attitude.
This shines interesting light on the historical record of social class
in ancient China.
Traditional subjects were persons of learned, royal or mystical
backgrounds.

One interesting feature of note, is the depiction of the most important person in the painting. You often see this person painted
much larger than the rest, such as the portrait of an emperor with
servants at right.

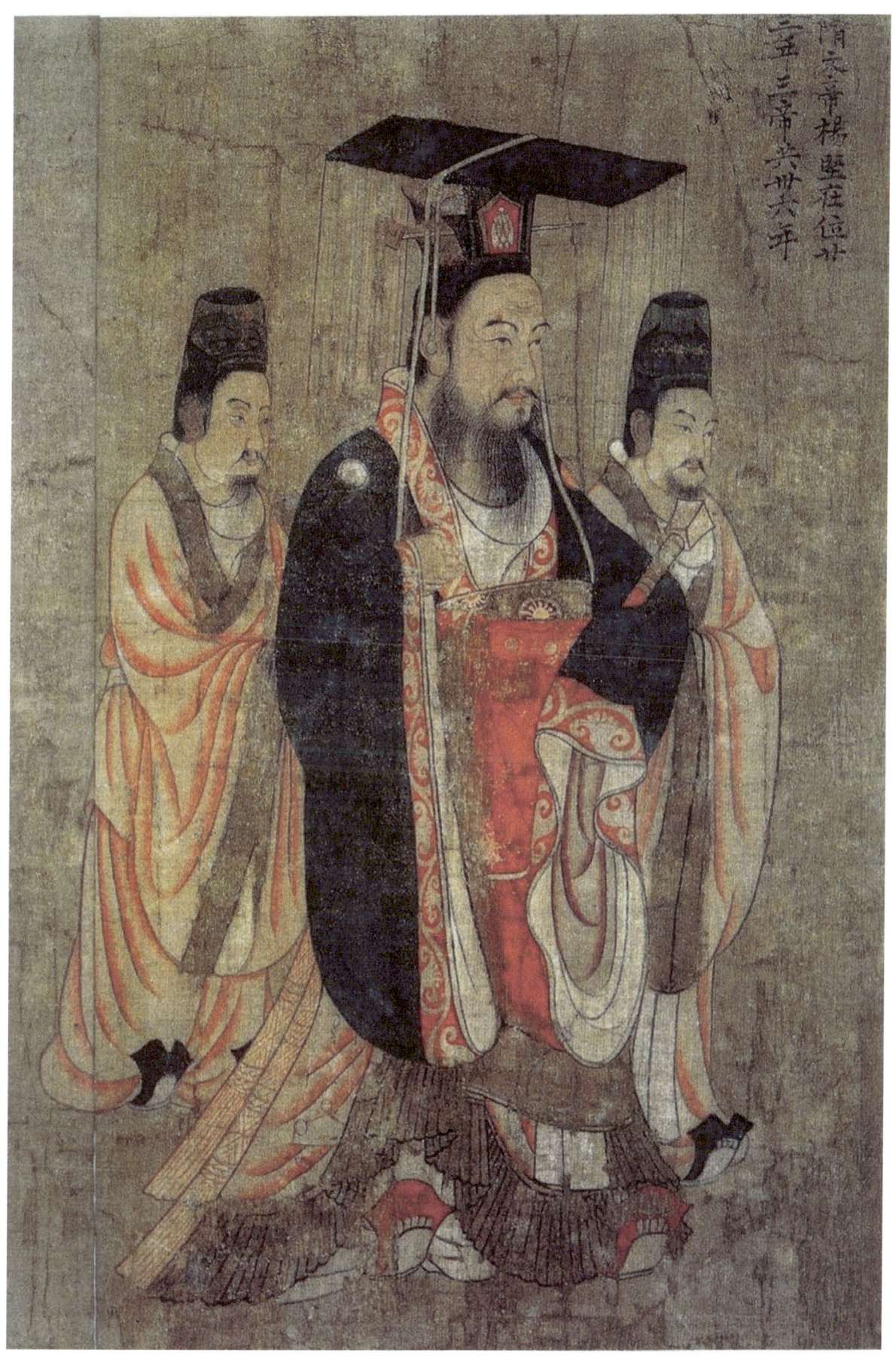

隋文帝楊堅在位廿
二年三帝六州六年

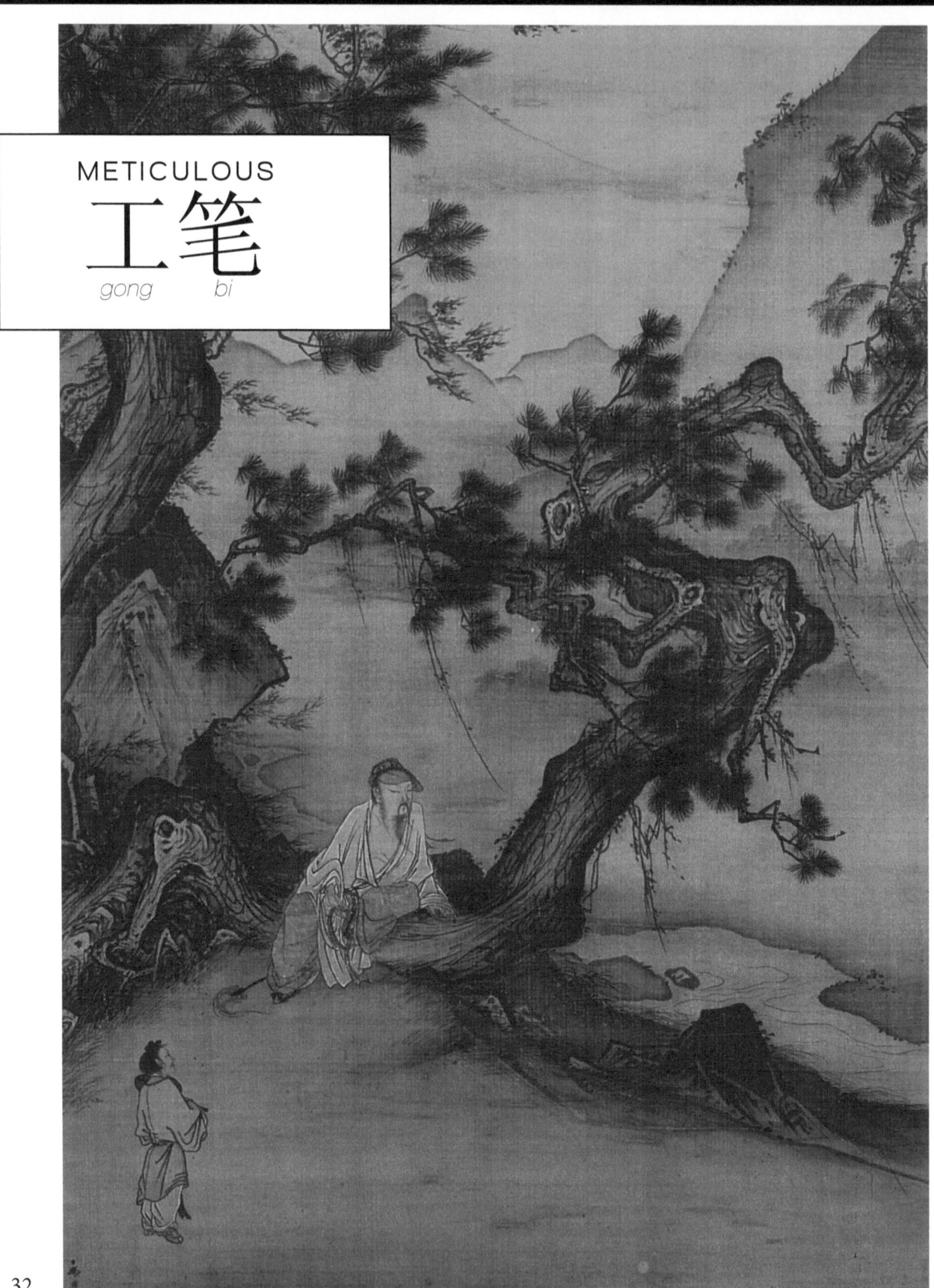

METICULOUS

工笔

gong   *bi*

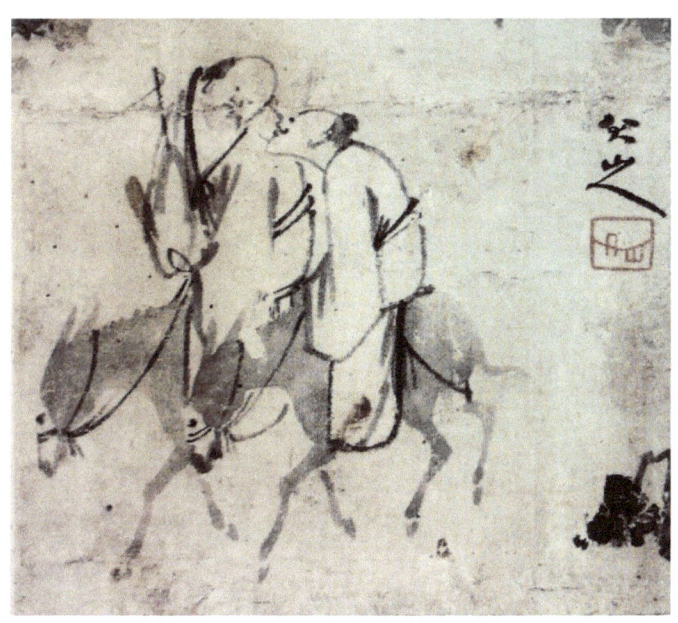

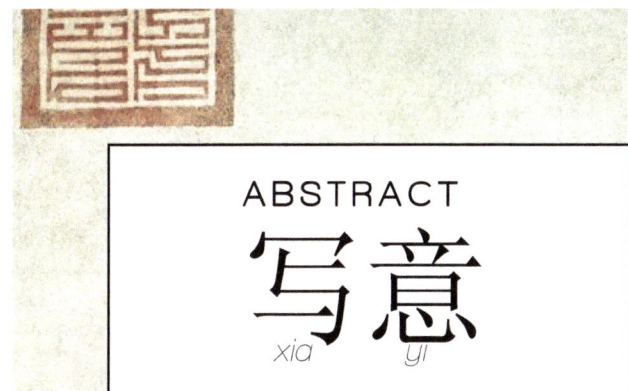

ABSTRACT

写意

xia　　*yi*

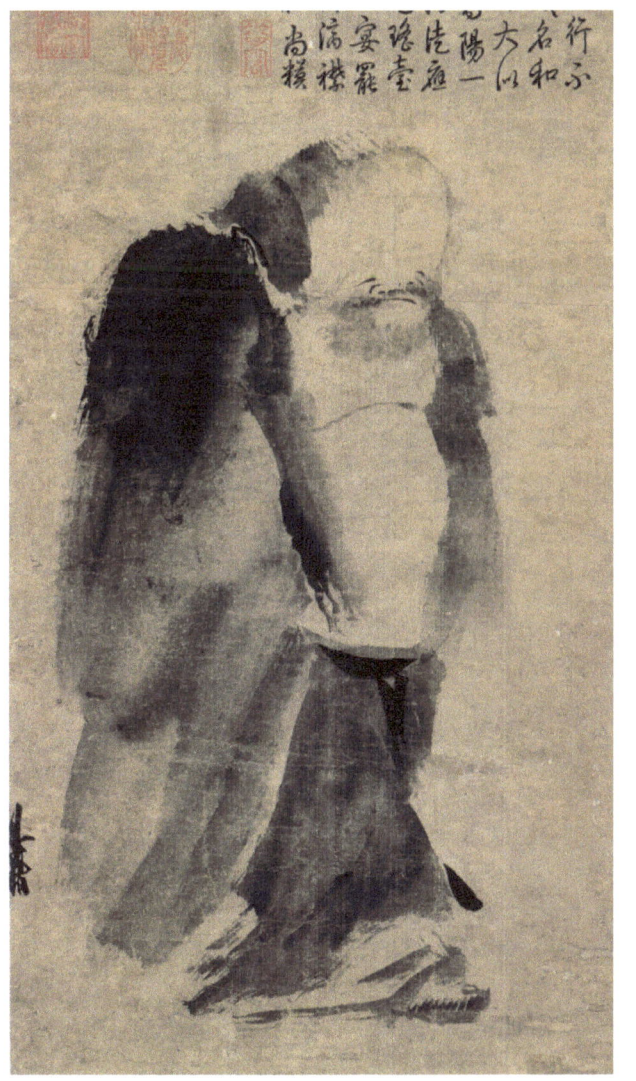

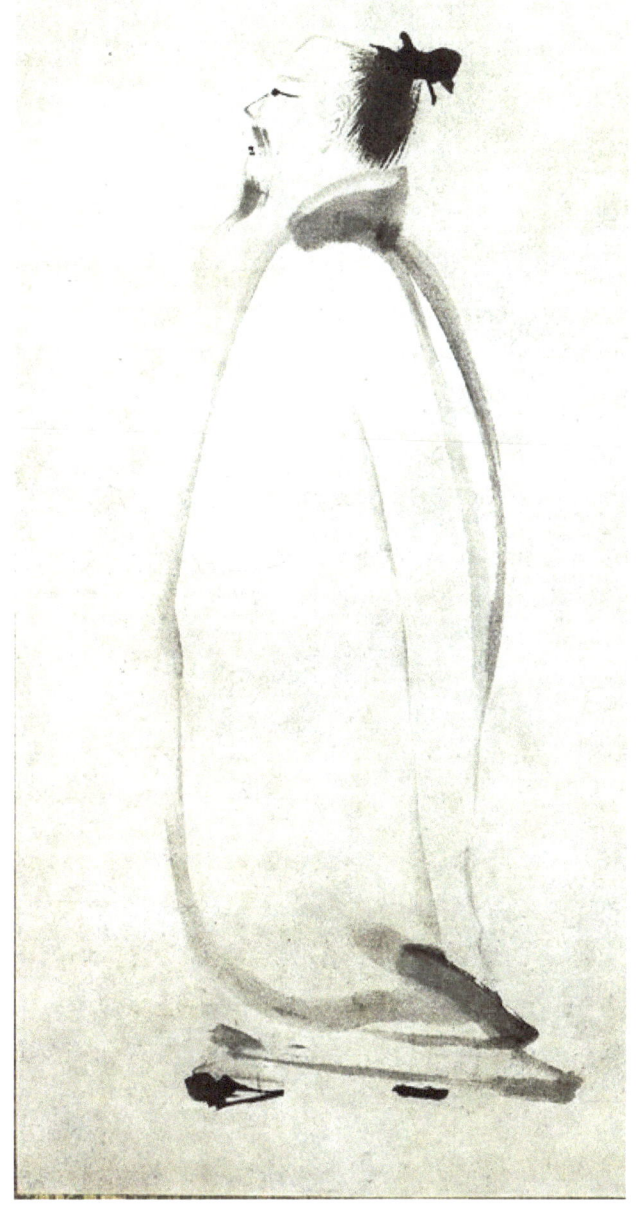

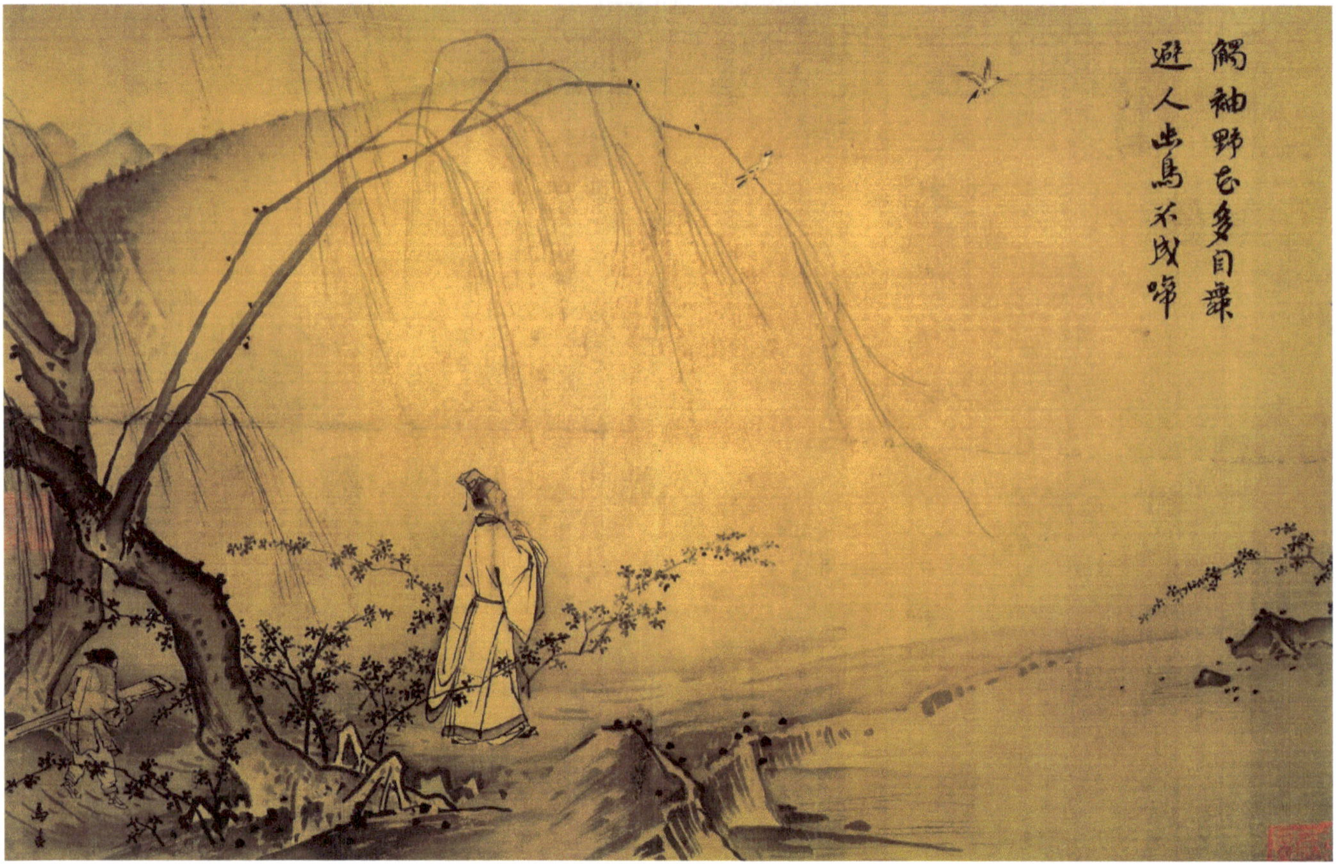

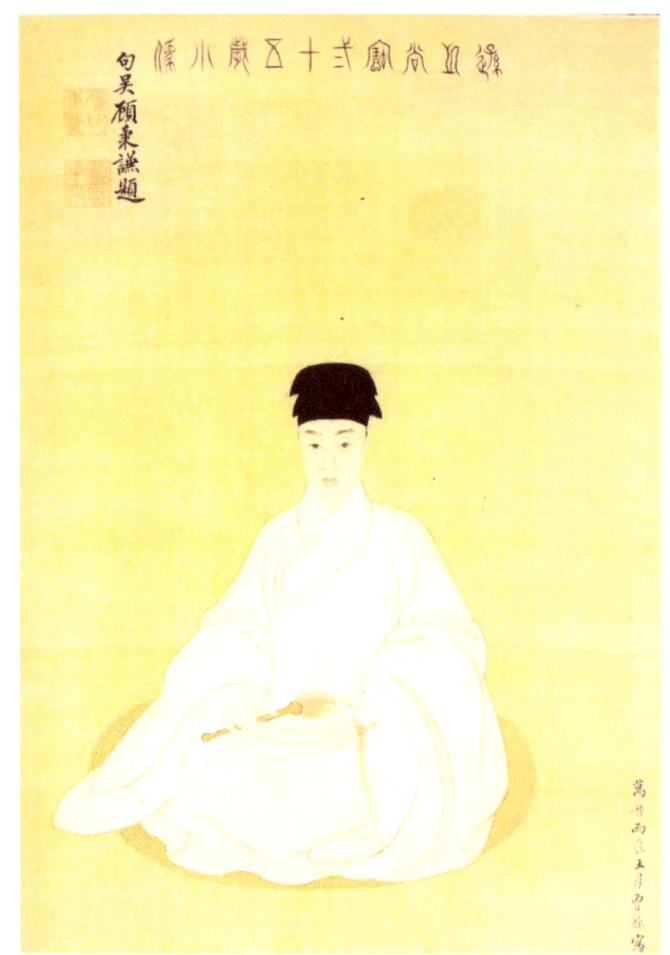

Above: *Walking on Path in Spring,* by Ma Yuan (馬遠) 1160-1225 AD

Right: *A Portrait of Wang Shimin* by Zeng Jing (曾鯨), who specialized in portrait painting during the Ming Dynasty 1368–1644 AD

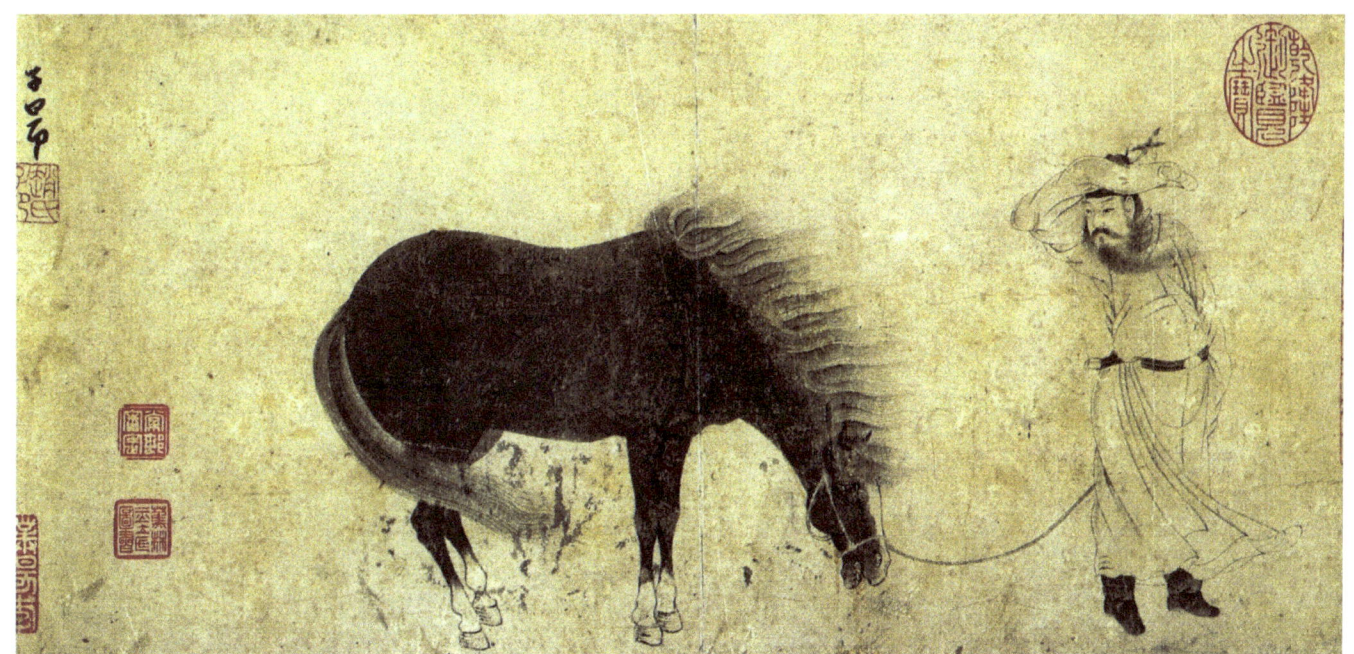

Royal Horses: Prized possessions, horses were symbols of wealth in ancient China and often depicted with people in lavish scenes such as the painting below titled: *Spring Outing of the Tang Court*, from the 8th century.

Examples are also seen in fine portrait form, such as the one above that seems to record bloodlines or a special animal.

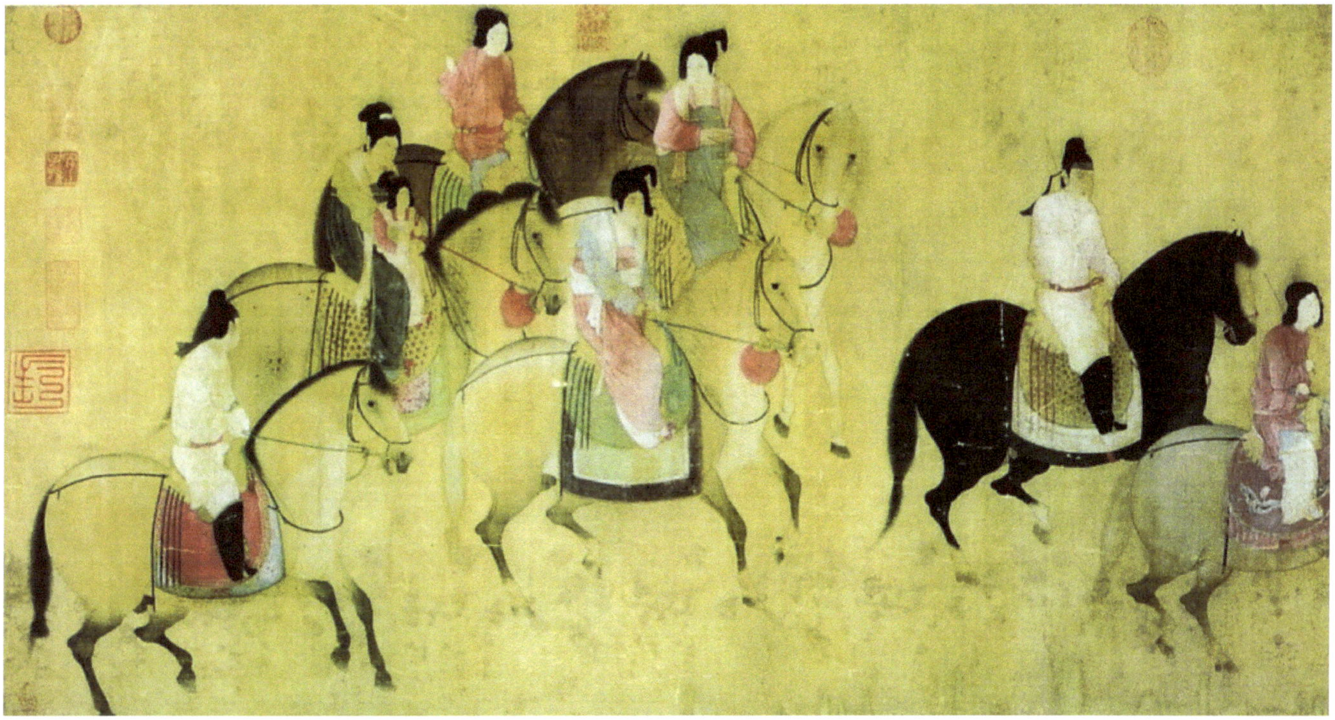

书法

CHINESE CALLIGRAPHY

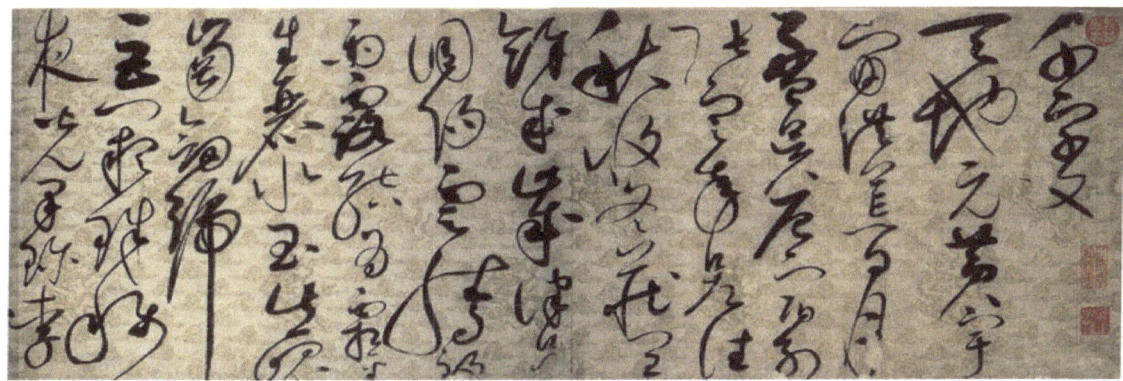

Have you ever gazed at a work of Chinese calligraphy and thought, "It looks pretty, but is hard to understand, I wish I knew more about calligraphy"? If so, you have expressed the most common reaction to this multifaceted art form.

Like western calligraphic styles or even fonts and typefaces, Chinese calligraphy brings feeling to written information. The use of Chinese characters to convey ideas rather then phonetic sounds makes Chinese calligraphy more powerful then its western counterparts.

There are many styles and forms of calligraphy that have evolved from ancient written forms of the Chinese language. Once used as a means of communication it is now treated mainly as form of artistic expression. Its widespread popularity crosses all demographics. It is enjoyed by many types of people, a testament to its ability to capture the imagination and stimulate the senses.

Presented here are the five basic styles of Chinese calligraphy. Recognizing the style is a good place to start when viewing a piece of calligraphy. You also get a feel for an artist's personality in their brushwork, finding varying amounts of strength and beauty in the strokes.

STYLES

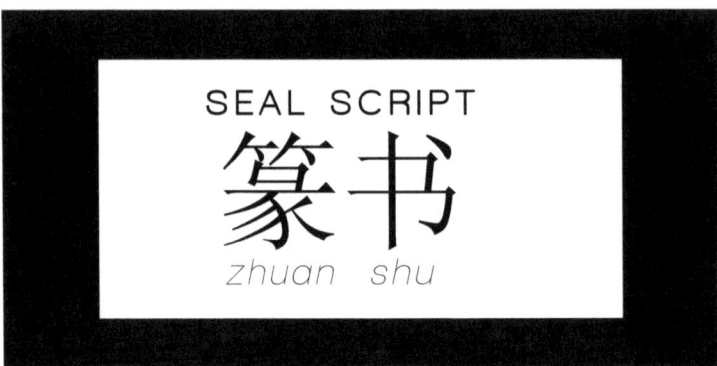

SEAL SCRIPT
篆书
zhuan shu

Seal script is the oldest of the popular forms of calligraphy. It developed from what is considered the first written form of Chinese, called the Turtle Shell script.

Seal script is not legible to most people outside of those who deliberately study it. However, its characters are often pictographic and it's possible to figure out what some of them mean with a little practice. Seal script also contains traces of modern characters as would be expected of this great-granddaddy to modern Chinese.

Its most common use is in making engraved seals, hence the name "seal script". It has a beautiful uniform quality and it is amazing that such an old writing system is still used and understood today.

Left:
Through 500-200 BC seal script was the most popular writing style in China. Incredibly it is still in use today!

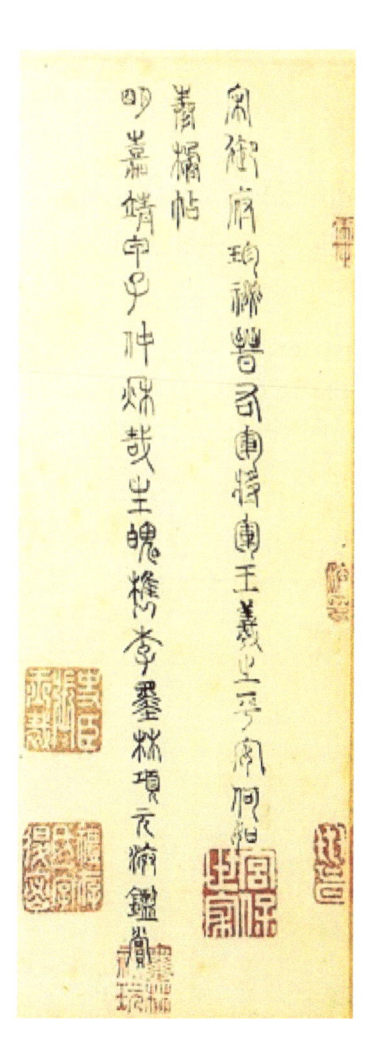

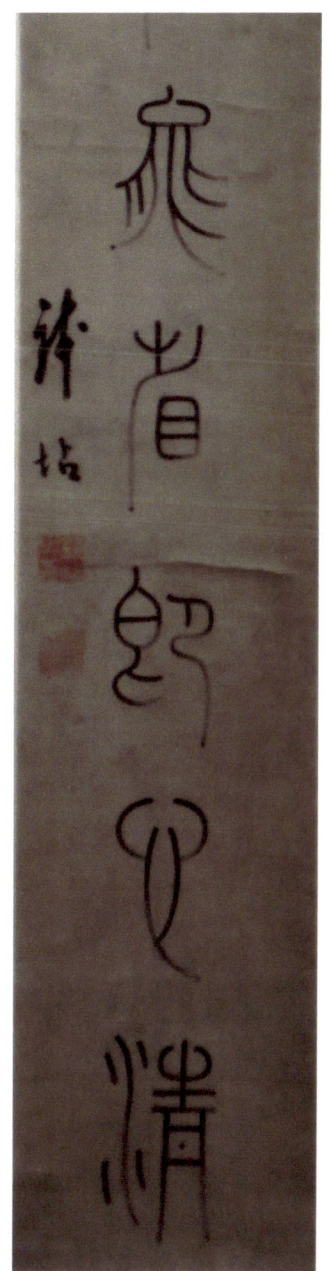

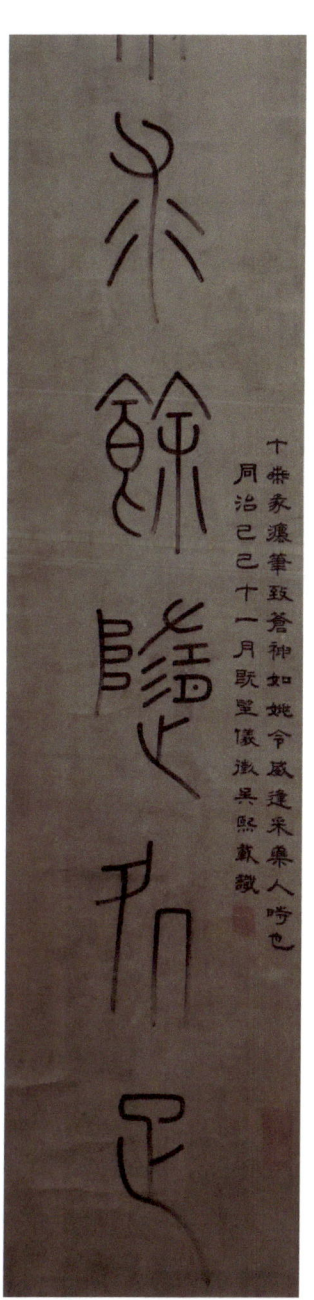

府 自 兌 廷

同治己巳十一月題聖儀澂吳熙載觀

STYLES

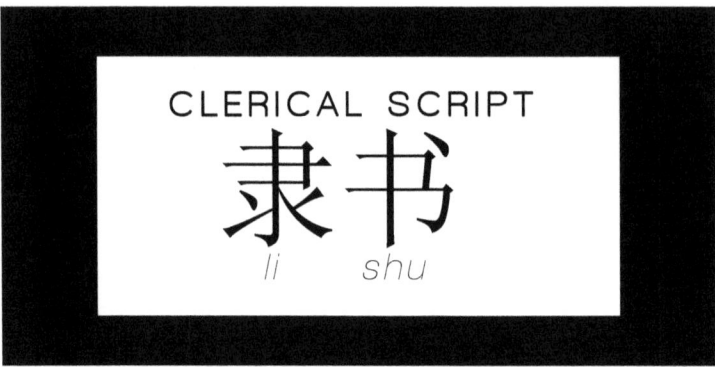

Clerical script is characterized by wide characters, special horizontal and downward right falling strokes and a dignified refined appearance.

Li shu is oriented to be written in well defined "squares" just like modern Chinese characters, however a side by side comparison reveals clerical script to be rectangular-wide, while regular script is rectangular-tall, generally speaking.

Very legible to modern Chinese readers *li shu* is popularly used in advertising and as the choice writing for "old fashioned" signs often mounted above the entryway to shops and hotels.

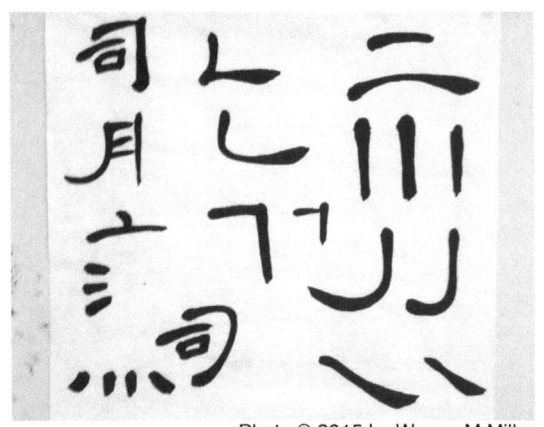

Left:
Deconstructed
strokes of *li shu*

40

Photo © 2015 by Wayne M Miller

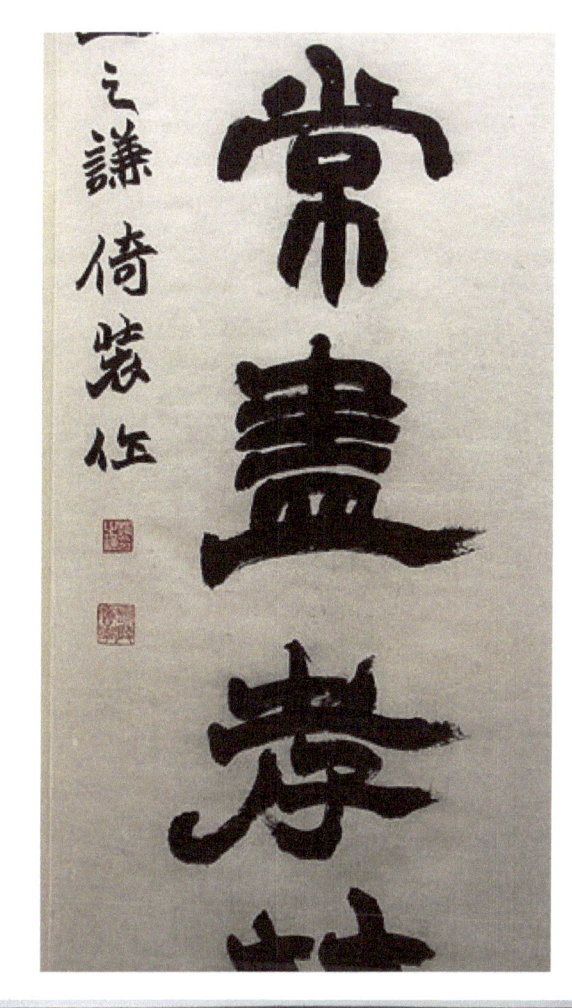

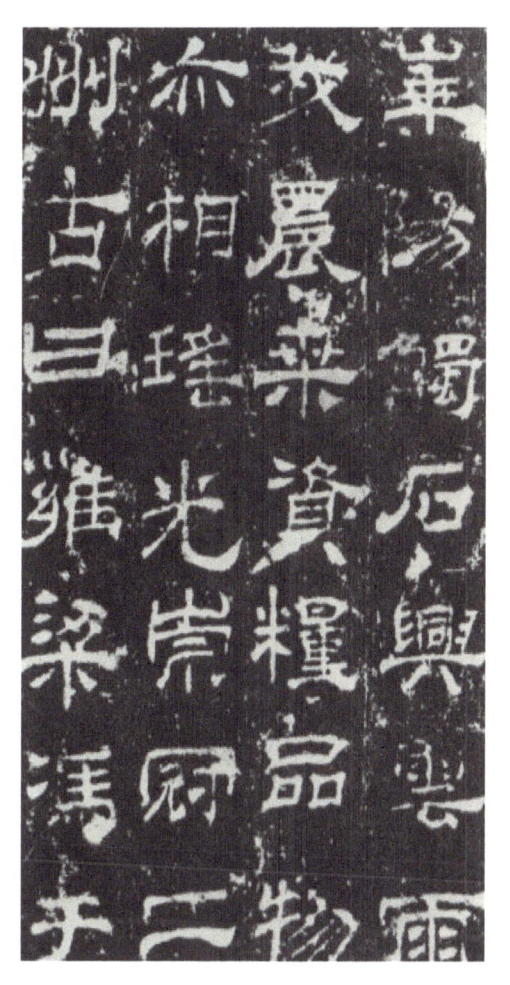

散慮逍遙 欣奏累遣 慼謝歡招 渠荷的歷 園莽抽條 枇杷晚翠 梧桐早凋 陳根委翳 落葉飄颻 游鵾獨運 凌摩絳霄 耽讀翫市 寓目囊箱 易輶攸畏 屬耳垣牆 具膳餐飯 適口充腸 飽飫烹宰 饑厭糟糠 親戚故舊 老少異糧 妾御績紡 侍巾帷房 紈扇圓潔 銀燭煒煌 晝眠夕寐 藍筍象床 弦歌酒讌 接杯舉觴 矯手頓足 悅豫且康 嫡後嗣續 祭祀烝嘗 稽顙再拜 悚懼恐惶 牋牒簡要 顧答審詳 骸垢想浴 執熱願涼 驢騾犢特 駭躍超驤 誅斬賊盜 捕獲叛亡 布射僚丸 嵇琴阮嘯 恬筆倫紙 鈞巧任釣 釋紛利俗 並皆佳妙 毛施淑姿 工顰妍笑 年矢每催 曦暉朗曜 璇璣懸斡 晦魄環照 指薪修祜 永綏吉劭 矩步引領 俯仰廊廟 束帶矜莊 徘徊瞻眺 孤陋寡聞 愚蒙等誚 謂語助者 焉哉乎也

STYLES

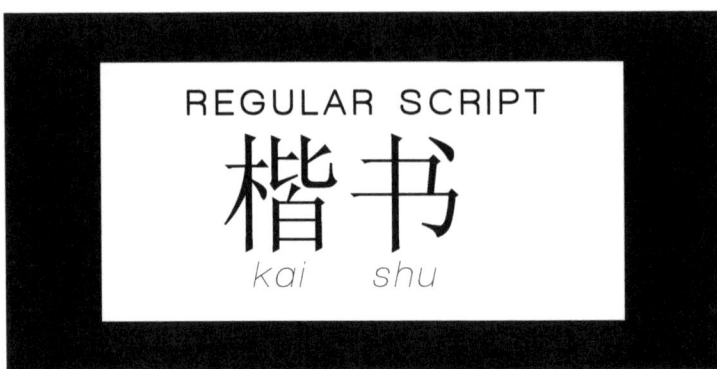

Kai shu directly translates "model script" and due to its use and widespread popularity it has become the standard and most recognized script of calligraphy, hence the name "regular script".

Its characteristics are easily recognizable: wedge-like tapers and fine points, with varying degrees of thick and thin strokes, all neatly balanced on a square space.

It should be noted that while mainland China uses simplified regular script, traditional characters are still exclusively used in the arts.

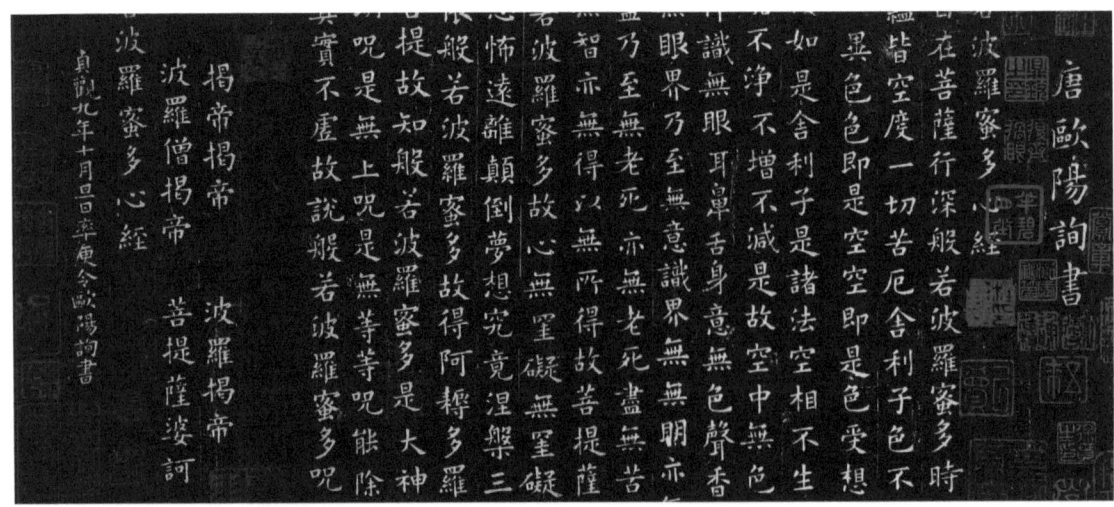

唐太祖武德四年置修文館於門下省九年
改曰宏文館丞太宗貞觀元年詔京官職事
五品以上子嗜書二十四人隸館習書出禁
中書法授之云者

朱汝珍

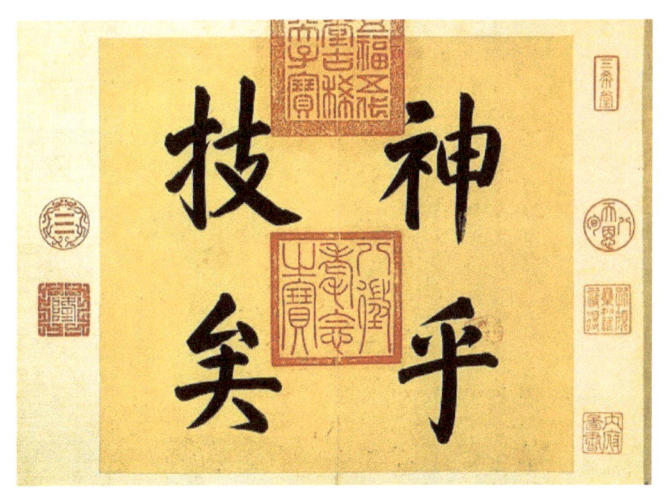

神平
技矣

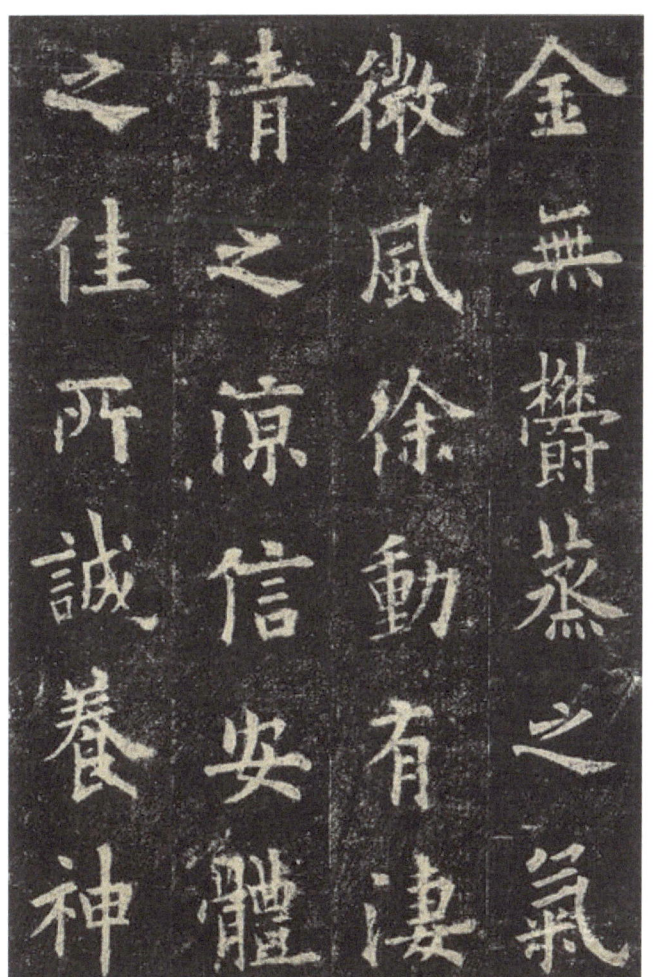

金無齏蒸之氣
微風徐動有淒
清之涼信安
之佳所誠養神

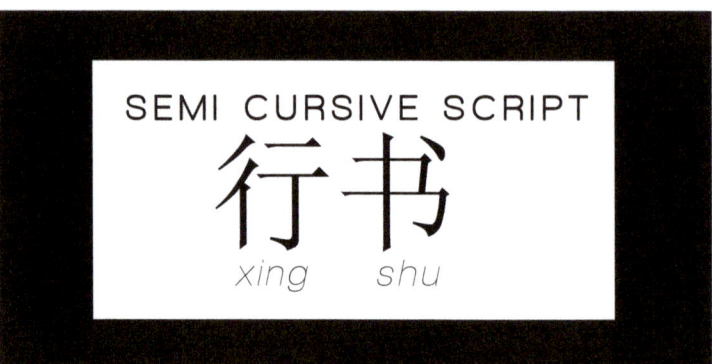

Semi-cursive speeds the process of writing by stringing strokes together and by abbreviation. It evolved out of clerical script around 100 AD.

Xing shu is often seen in inscriptions or poems on Chinese paintings. Often the brushwork an artist uses in his writing style matches his painting. The keen eye of an experienced artist quickly spots such similarities.

BELOW:
An 11th century painting and semi-cursive poem by Jhao Ji (趙佶）
Titled: *Dragon Stone*

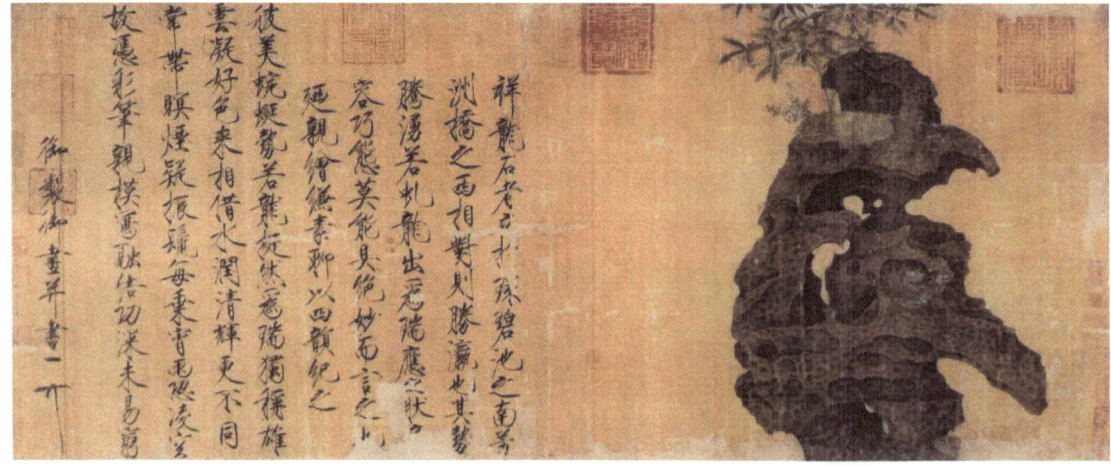

永和九年歲在癸丑暮春之初會于會稽山陰之蘭亭脩稧事也群賢畢至少長咸集此地有崇山峻領茂林脩竹又有清流激湍映帶左右引以為流觴曲水列坐其次雖無絲竹管弦之盛一觴一詠亦足以暢敘幽情是日也天朗氣清惠風和暢仰觀宇宙之大俯察品類之盛所以遊目騁懷足以極視聽之娛信可樂也夫人之相與俯仰一世或取諸懷抱悟言一室之內或因寄所託放浪形骸之外雖趣舍萬殊靜躁不同當其欣於所遇暫得於己快然自足不知老之將至及其所之既惓情隨事遷感慨係之矣向之所欣俛仰之間以為陳迹猶不能不以之興懷況脩短隨化終期於盡古人云死生亦大矣豈不痛哉每攬昔人興感之由若合一契未嘗不臨文嗟悼不能喻之於懷固知一死生為虛誕齊彭殤為妄作後之視今亦由今之視昔悲夫故列敘時人錄其所述雖世殊事異所以興懷其致一也後之攬者亦將有感於斯文

Right: *Duilian* (对联) is a form of presenting calligraphy on two long strips of paper. During Chinese holidays every doorframe is decorated with a phrase on either side, conveying auspicious sayings on red paper.

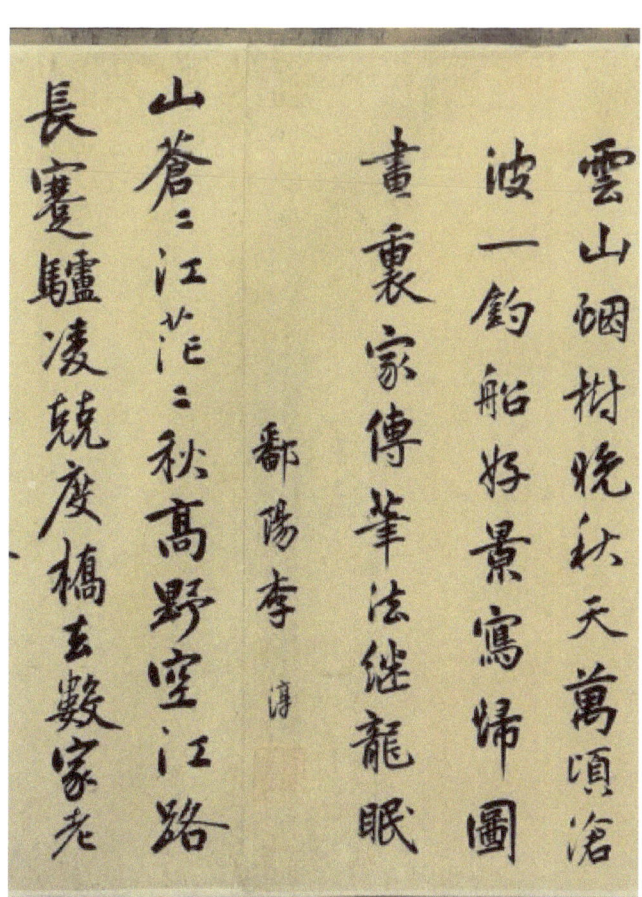

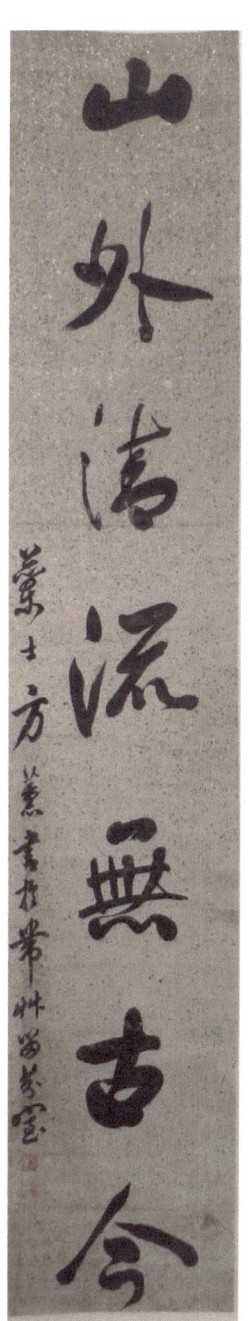

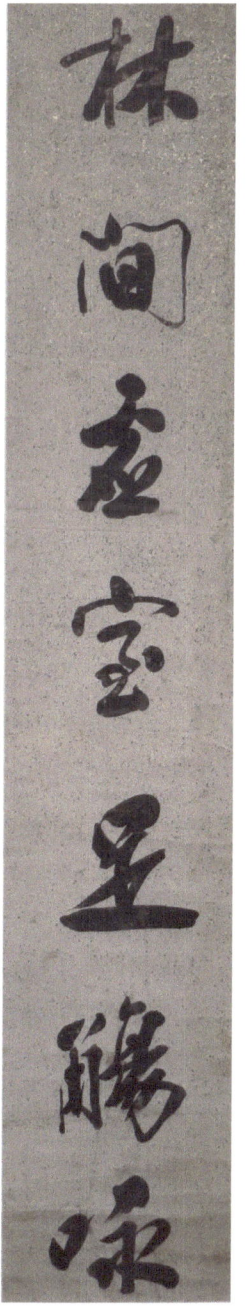

STYLES

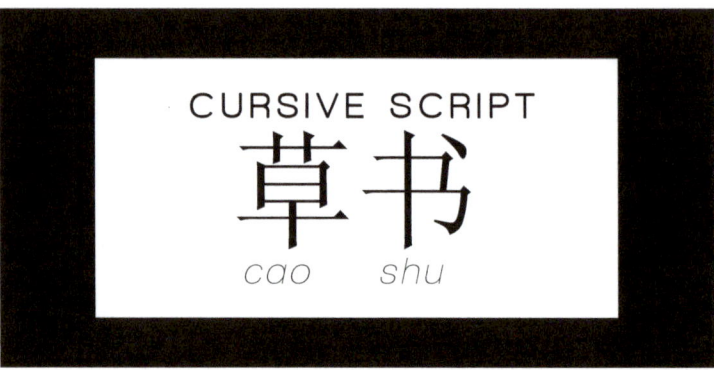

CURSIVE SCRIPT
草书
cao   shu

Cursive script drastically abbreviates, simplifies, and speeds up the writing process to the point that legibility deteriorates.

This style produces interesting artistic effects and also expresses much emotion in the brushwork. It takes into account pressure, speed, color, whether the ink is dry or wet, shape, size and configuration.

Of course these qualities are expressed in every script, but *cao shu* lends itself well to expressive aspects.

Easily recognized due to its haphazard nature and the running of strokes and even entire characters together. *Cao shu* translates as "sloppy script" or "grass script" and both names seem to describe this style well.

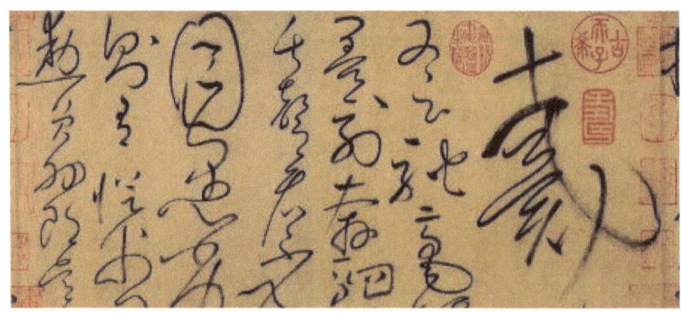

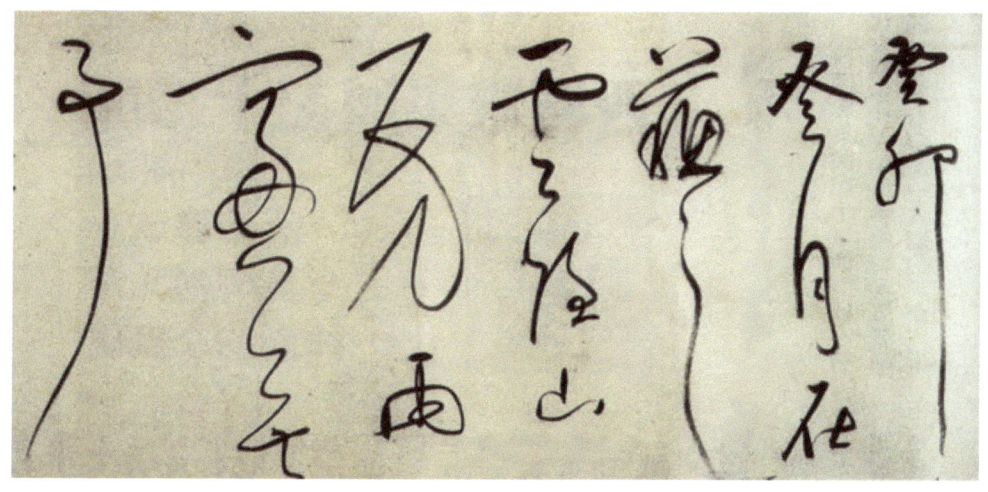

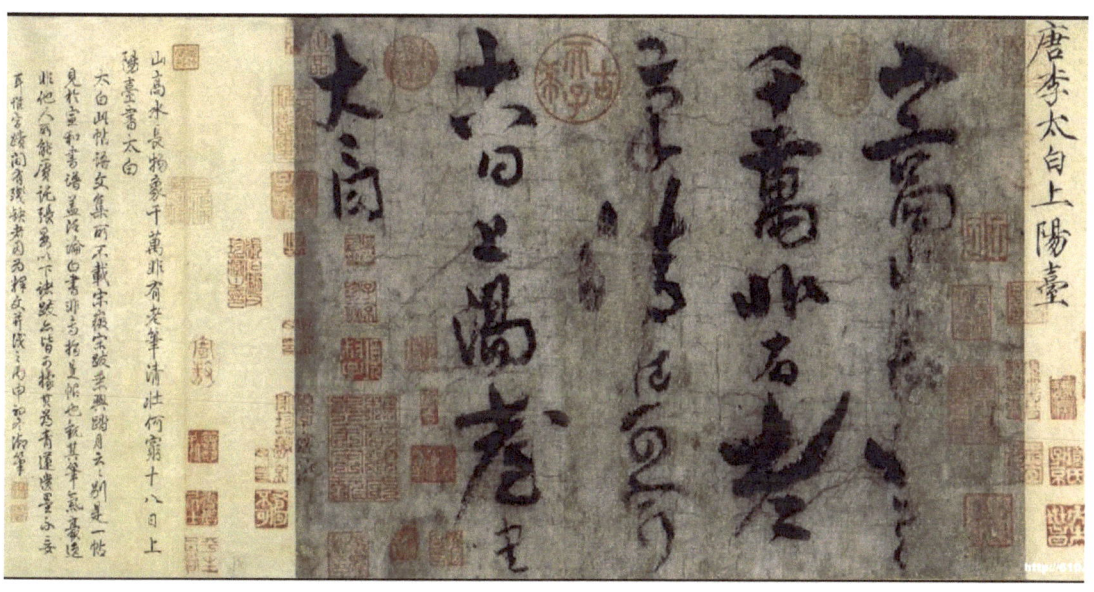

唐李太白上陽臺

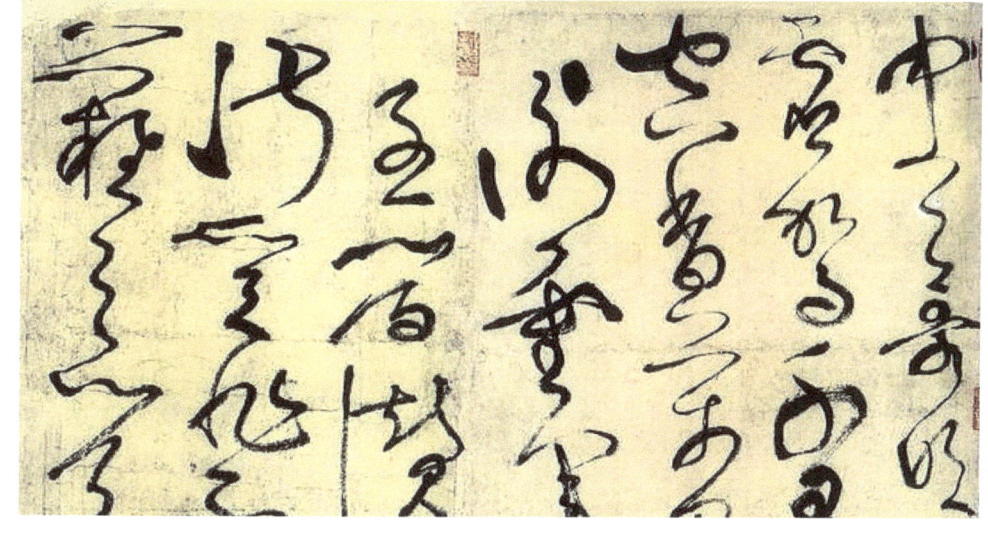

47

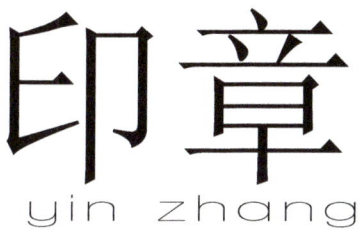

SIGNET SEALS

印章
yin zhang

Chinese culture frequently uses seals, even today a seal is legally binding and used by individuals, companies, governments and everything in-between. It is considered better than a signature and is stamped in bright "China red". Traditionally a cinnabar paste was used.

The high contrast of red seals with dark ink on white paper makes for a very pleasing visual effect in Chinese art and much thought is given to their use and placement.

Signet seals, commonly called "chops" come in all shapes and sizes and typically bear names, mottos, poems, and sometimes include pictures. Chops are engraved in hard surfaces with chisels. According with tradition, *zhuan shu* (seal script) is used, creating a very appealing decorative effect.

CHOPS

Seals are placed on finished artwork much like a signature, if only one seal is used it will be the artist's "name chop" incorporating their family name or "pen name" onto the art. In addition they may add a chop from their studio and perhaps a seal with a poetic phrase that accents the art.

Left:
If a single seal is used on finished artwork, it is the artist's "name chop".

Right:
Chops come in many shapes and styles. Typically signature seals are square.

Collectors, studios and museums may add their own chops to the piece to show it was in their possession. This is why many older famous paintings such as the one below, seem to be covered in seals. Interestingly, this does not detract from the value and can, in fact, increase it as the seals themselves may be famous or belong to a famous proprietor.

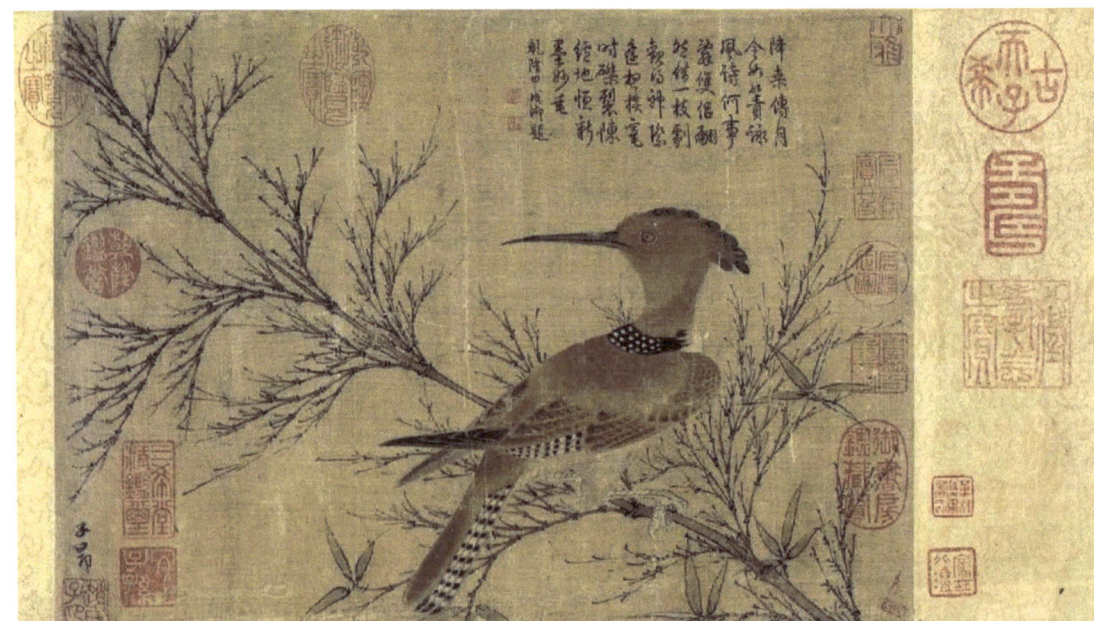

印章

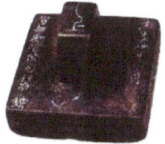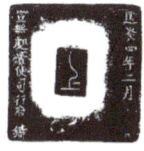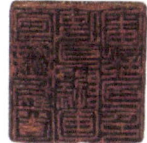

Right: Seal and seal paste, often intricately adorned and cut by specialized artisans, *yin zhang* are beautiful works of art in their own right.

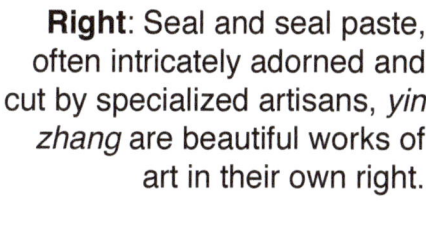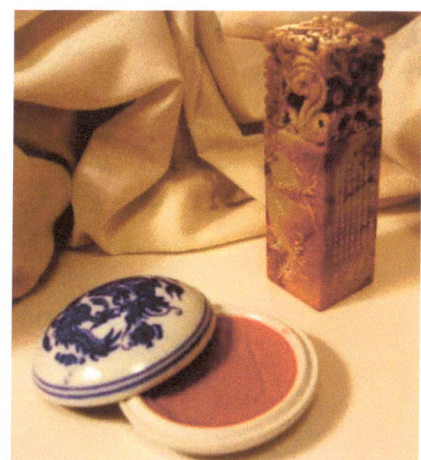

Above: *Song Dynasty governmental seal used around 1,000 yeas ago.*

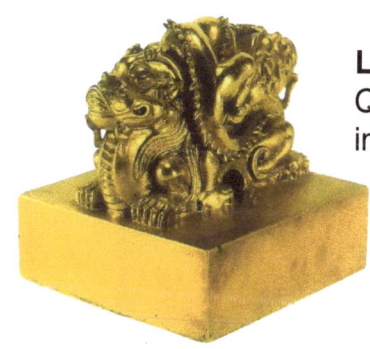

Left:
Qing Dynasty golden dragon imperial seal, 16th century AD.

Below, Adding a seal to a monochrome painting is said to be "adding the eye to the dragon".

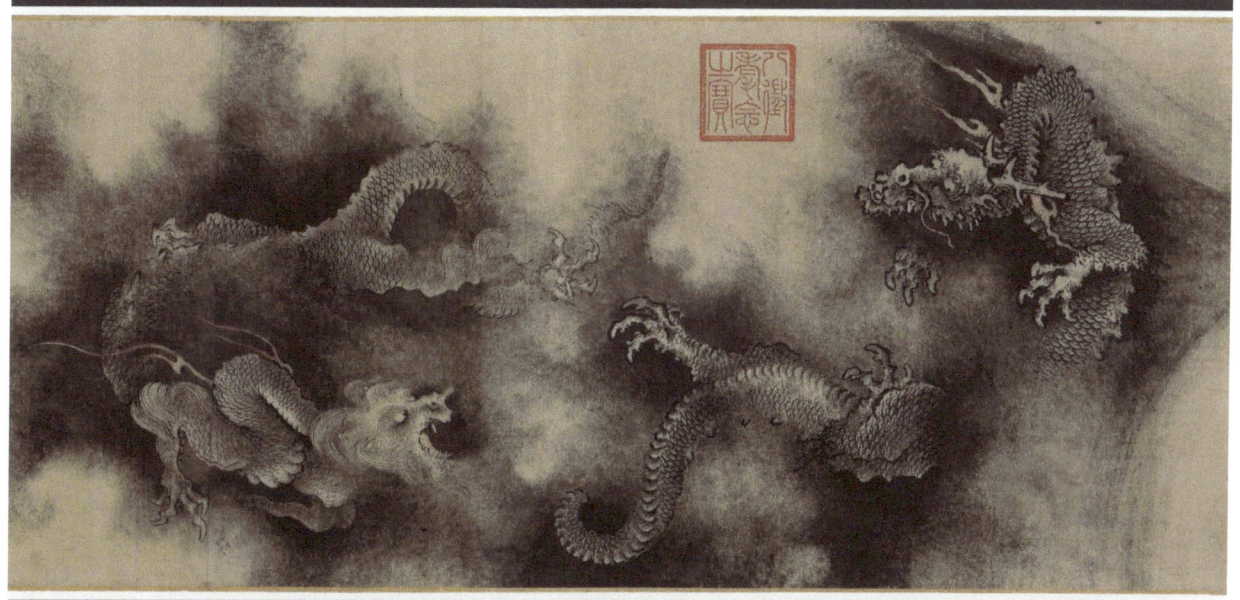

结束

IN CONCLUSION

Through this introduction, traditional Chinese art has been explored in thematic sections including formal and abstract painting styles, calligraphy, and signet seals. This representation is truly only a small taste of the essential flavors of this intriguing medium. Hopefully this taste has nourished your curiosity and inspired a better understanding of traditional Chinese art. Best of wishes to your artistic endeavors and many thanks to you for picking up and reading this book. ~Wayne Miller

Acknowledgments

Special thanks to Mike Lane for his inspiration and guidance in art, life and Christ centered faith. And to my teachers Mr. Huang and Mr. Lee for their patience and teaching spirit. As well, thanks to all those who shared their time, skills, and friendship with me. If you are reading this, you know who you are.

www.ingramcontent.com/pod-product-compliance
Lightning Source LLC
Chambersburg PA
CBHW051050180526
45172CB00002B/582